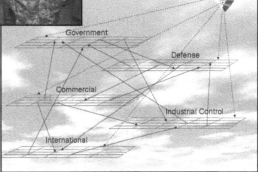

INFORMATION AS POWER

CHINA'S CYBER POWER
AND
AMERICA'S NATIONAL SECURITY

by
Colonel Jayson M. Spade

Edited by
Jeffrey L. Caton

U.S. ARMY WAR COLLEGE

U.S. ARMY WAR COLLEGE

INFORMATION AS POWER

CHINA'S CYBER POWER
AND
AMERICA'S NATIONAL SECURITY
by
Colonel Jayson M. Spade

Edited by
Jeffrey L. Caton

The Information in Warfare Group of the U.S. Army War College is proud to publish "China's Cyber Power and America's National Security" by Colonel Jayson M. Spade. This work is exceptionally well-researched and written as evidenced by its receipt of the Armed Forces Communications and Electronics Association (AFCEA) writing award in 2011.

Special thanks to Benjamin C. Leitzel for his significant editorial and administrative support, to Ritchie Dion and Elizabeth Heffner for their meticulous layout editing, and to Jennifer Nevil for the cover design.

CHINA'S CYBER POWER AND AMERICA'S NATIONAL SECURITY

China's Cyber Power and America's National Security

by

Colonel Jayson M. Spade

CHINA'S CYBER POWER AND
AMERICA'S NATIONAL SECURITY

by

Colonel Jayson M. Spade
United States Army

Edited by:
Jeffrey L. Caton

Executive Agent for the Mongraph:
United States Army War College

The views contained in this publication are those expressed by the authors and do not necessarily reflect the official policy or position of the United States Army War College, the Department of Defense, or any other Department or Agency within the United States Government. This publication is cleared for public release; distribution is unlimited.

Published May 2012.

This publication is available on line at the following:

http://www.carlisle.army.mil/dime or,

http://www.csl.army.mil/InfoAsPower.aspx

Cover photograph by Staff Sgt. DeNoris A. Mickle, USAF. Used by permission.

U.S. ARMY WAR COLLEGE
CARLISLE BARRACKS, PENNSYLVANIA 17013

PREFACE

The Information in Warfare Group of the U.S. Army War College is proud to publish "China's Cyber Power and America's National Security" by Colonel Jayson M. Spade. This effort represents the first research paper published outside the annual "Information as Power" student anthology as a stand-alone monograph. There are several reasons for this distinction. Spade's work is exceptionally well-researched and written as evidenced by its receipt of the Armed Forces Communications and Electronics Association (AFCEA) writing award in 2011. Additionally, the topic of cyber power and national security remains a wicked U.S. national security problem that requires thoughtful and scholarly discourse toward a possible solution. To that end, Spade masterfully pushes the body of knowledge forward in this paper.

Originally submitted as a Strategy Research Project, this monograph examines the growth of Chinese cyber power and their known and demonstrated capabilities for offensive, defensive and exploitive computer network operations. Comparing China's capacity and potential to the United States' current efforts for cyber security, Spade highlights the degree to which the People's Republic of China's cyber power poses a threat to United States' national security and offers proposals to improve future U.S. policy for cyber security and defense.

Like the "Information as Power" student anthology, this paper provides a resource for U.S. Army War College graduates, senior military officers, and national security practitioners concerned with the information element of power. It is indicative of importance of the Army as a learning organization that values soldier-scholars like Colonel Spade.

Professor Dennis M. Murphy
Director, Information in Warfare Group
United States Army War College
Carlisle, Pennsylvania

CHINA'S CYBER POWER AND AMERICA'S NATIONAL SECURITY

Information warfare is entirely different from the conventional concept of aiming at a target and annihilating it with bullets, or of commanders relying on images and pictures obtained by visual detection and with remote-sensing equipment to conduct operations....The multidimensional, interconnected networks on the ground, in the air (or outer space), and under water, as well as terminals, modems, and software, are not only instruments, but also weapons. A people's war under such conditions would be complicated, broad-spectrum, and changeable, with higher degrees of uncertainty and probability, which requires full preparation and circumspect organization.

— Wei Jincheng, "Information War: A New Form of People's War"
Liberation Army Daily[1]

IN TERMS OF MILITARY CAPABILITIES, the United States has been the world's only superpower since 1991. In future conflicts, adversaries who cannot match U.S. military capabilities will necessarily look for asymmetric means to counter America's strength.[2] As demonstrated in the 1991 Gulf War and the 2003 invasion of Iraq, information technology is critical to America's military superiority in areas such as command, control, and communications; intelligence gathering, surveillance, and reconnaissance; logistics, transportation, and administration. This reliance on information technology might prove to be America's asymmetric Achilles' heel.

Cyber power, the employment of computer network attack and computer network exploitation, is a relatively inexpensive but potentially effective means by which an adversary might counter U.S. military power. And the potential for cyber power is not limited to use in a direct fight with America's military. Military power is one facet of national power, which also includes the economy as well as political and national will. The United States as a whole – the government and civil sector – is dependent on cyberspace and information systems for many routine and daily functions. America's highly networked society, using an

Internet designed for open and easy information exchange, could be subject to cyber attack in 21st century cyber warfare.[3]

Since 1991, the People's Republic of China has increasingly funded, developed, acquired, and fielded advanced cyber technology in its government, military and civil sectors. This is a holistic effort to build China's political and economic power. It is also a deliberate attempt to develop a cyber warfare capability as an asymmetric means to fight and defeat the United States' superior military power. The Chinese recognize that cyberspace can be a war fighting domain and that cyber power now ranks with land, sea, and air power in terms of military strength, victory or defeat.[4]

The People's Liberation Army (PLA) is preparing for total cyber warfare. They are conducting cyberspace reconnaissance; creating the ability to do economic harm and damage critical infrastructure; preparing to disrupt communications and information systems necessary to support conventional armed conflict; and readying to conduct psychological operations to influence the will of the American people.[5] The People's Republic of China is one of the world's leading cyber powers and is working steadily with the intent to develop the capacity to deter or defeat the United States fighting in and through cyberspace. Given these facts, how should the United States' national security structure change to address the evolving strength of China in cyberspace? This paper examines the growth of Chinese cyber power; their known and demonstrated cyber capabilities; and how they might use cyber power in support of Chinese national security objectives. By comparing China's cyber capacity and potential to the United States' cyber security capabilities, this paper examines the degree to which China's cyber power threatens American national security and then offers proposals to improve U.S. policy for cyber security and defense.

Cyberspace: Increasing Dependence, Increasing Threat

One could argue that cyberspace was born in 1969 through the efforts of the Advanced Research Projects Agency (ARPA). The ARPANET project aimed to network geographically separated computers to allow research contractors to exchange information more efficiently. It began modestly, linking civilian and military researchers through computers at Stanford Research Institute, the University of California at Los Angeles and Santa Barbara, and the University of Utah. The first message consisted of three letters and the receiving computer crashed after the third letter.[6] Despite this inauspicious beginning there were 13 computers on ARPAnet in 1970, 57 computers in 1975, and 213 computers by 1981, with more computers connecting roughly every 20 days.[7] By 2010, over 77 percent of the American population actively used the Internet for business, research, education, communication, and entertainment.[8]

In 40 years, cyberspace activity has expanded exponentially and permeated almost every dimension of human interaction. It is an immeasurable network of smaller networks used by government, business, research institutions, and individuals around the world. Americans depend on information technology (IT) and the Internet for news and information, work and personal communication, banking transactions and investments, shopping, travel, and social networking. Globally, almost two billion people use the Internet, a 400 percent increase from 2000 to 2010.[9] Globalization is dependent on people's ability to interact in cyberspace, using online networks to enable the exchange of information, goods, and services around the world.[10]

As cyberspace use has increased, so has misuse of cyberspace. In the last 10 years, world-wide incidents of cyber attacks[11] have escalated, in both government and private sectors. Some attacks are cyber crime, using the Internet to generate illegal financial profit.[12] Some are purely malicious, such as a hacker releasing a virus into the Internet. But there is an increasing trend for cyber attacks to play a part in international state-versus-state conflict. When U.S. aircraft accidently bombed China's Belgrade Embassy in 1999, Chinese hackers defaced U.S. government websites and American hackers responded in kind. This situation repeated itself in May 2001 when a U.S. Navy P-3 Orion collided with a People's Liberation Army Navy (PLAN) F-8 fighter. Hacker-wars accompanied NATO's intervention in Kosovo, Israel's 2006 incursion into Lebanon, and the Russian conflict in Chechnya.[13]

The degree of governmental complicity in hacker activity is hotly debated. In 2007, when the government of Estonia moved a World War II Soviet monument contrary to the wishes of the Russian government, a massive distributed denial of service (DDoS) attack blocked Estonia's access to cyberspace.[14] Shortly before Russia invaded Georgia in 2008, Georgia suffered a DDoS attack that shut down its Internet access. In both cases, the Russian government denied involvement, attributing the attacks to the actions of 'patriotic hackers.'[15] While this attribution is partially true, there is evidence that the Russian government enabled and abetted the hackers, using methods that allowed the government plausible deniability.[16]

The People's Republic of China (PRC) is prominent among countries employing cyber attacks and intrusion against other nations. Taiwan is a perennial favorite for PRC-based cyber attacks. The first 'Taiwan-China Hacker War' erupted in 1999 when the President of Taiwan suggested state-to-state relations between the island and mainland. Chinese hackers responded by defacing Taiwan government, university and commercial sites. In 2003, mainland hackers penetrated networks in 30 Taiwan government agencies, including the Defense Ministry, Election Commission, National Police Administration, and many Taiwan companies. In 2004 hackers infiltrated the Ministry of Finance and Kuomintang Party. In 2005, the Taiwan National Security Council was targeted with socially engineered emails[17] containing malicious code.[18]

China's cyber activities are not limited to Taiwan; they are global. In May 2007, Trojan horse[19] programs sent terabytes[20] of information from government networks at the German Chancellery and their foreign, economic and research ministries to what officials believe were PLA-supported servers in Lanzhou and Beijing. Security officials estimate 40 percent of all German companies have been targeted by state-sponsored Internet espionage, most coming from either China or Russia.[21] In November 2007, the United Kingdom's Director-General of MI5[22] sent a confidential letter warning 300 chief executives and security chiefs at banks, accounting and legal firms of electronic espionage by "Chinese state organizations." These attacks used Trojans customized to defeat the firms' IT security systems and exfiltrate confidential data.[23] In March 2009, the University of Toronto's Munk Center for International Studies exposed a cyber espionage ring that had penetrated more than 1,200 computer systems in 103 countries.

Targets included news media, government ministries and embassies, and nongovernmental and international organizations. Dubbed 'Ghostnet' by the investigating team, these computer network exploitations (CNE) used Chinese malware and three of the four control servers were in Chinese provinces.[24]

China has repeatedly targeted the United States. In 2004, a CNE exfiltrated terabytes of data from Sandia Laboratories,[25] the National Air and Space Administration, and several U.S. defense contractors. Code-named *Titan Rain*, this CNE routed the data through servers in South Korea, Hong Kong, and Taiwan before sending it to China.[26] In August 2006, a CNE originating from China infiltrated computer systems belonging to Members of Congress and the House Foreign Affairs Committee. Congressman Frank Wolf (R-VA) maintains that "critical and sensitive information about U.S. foreign policy and the work of Congress" was exfiltrated.[27] In October 2006, computer network attacks launched from Chinese servers forced the Commerce Department's Bureau of Industry and Security (BIS) to block Internet access for over a month. BIS replaced hundred computers to expunge their network of all malicious code.[28] Between 2007 and 2009, a CNE exfiltrated data on Lockheed Martin's F-35 fighter program. Forensics found that the intruders searched for data on the plane's design, performance statistics, and electronic systems. Investigators traced the CNE to Chinese Internet protocol addresses[29] used in previous network intrusions.[30]

Cyberspace, Cyber Power & Cyber War

For most of human history, people lived, worked, and waged war in two physical domains: land and sea. In 1903 mankind added air to its accessible domains and, in 1957, added the space domain. All these domains exist in nature; cyberspace is the first manmade domain. While one could argue that the world has lived with and in cyberspace for four decades, the term itself, 'cyberspace,' has been widely and variously defined, understood, and misunderstood.[31] According to the 2008 *National Security Presidential Directive 54/Homeland Security Presidential Directive 23*, cyberspace is "the interdependent network of information technology infrastructures, and includes the Internet, telecommunications networks, computer systems, and embedded processors and controllers in critical industries. Common usage of the term also refers to the virtual environment of information and interactions between people."[32]

Cyberspace is both a physical and virtual domain. The physical part is the millions of networked information and communication technologies that create and enable it: computers, servers, routers, processors, satellites, switches, and cables. The virtual part is formed by electronic connections and by the data sent between and stored in the pieces of its physical infrastructure. It exists globally, created and transmitted, stored and maintained by governments, public and private owners. Cyberspace changes and evolves as people develop new hardware and software technology. It is pervasive, transcending organizational boundaries and geopolitical borders and readily accessible to almost anyone from almost anywhere in the world. From a military perspective, cyberspace both enables operations in the other four domains and is a domain in which operations can be conducted.[33]

For national defense and national power, nation-states have developed military capabilities for each of the natural domains: sea power (navies), land power (armies), air power (air and air defense forces), and space power (spacecraft and satellites). The purpose of these powers is for the nation-state to establish control and exert influence within and through the domains, control and influence being steps toward the state achieving its national goals and objectives. States create armies to control, defend, and extend their borders; navies to protect their coasts, control sea lanes, and attack others' by sea; air and outer space forces to attack through the sky, defend against like attacks, and conduct observation. Each of these powers is intended to use a domain to the advantage of the state.[34] And each of these powers can support and reinforce the powers dominant in the other domains. Land power protects the ports and airfields from which sea and air power originates. Air and space power provides overhead protection for land and sea power. Air and sea power enables land power projection. While designed to operate primarily in its own domain, each of the powers can exert influence into the other domains.

Cyber power is the ability of a nation-state to establish control and exert influence within and through cyberspace, in support of and in conjunction with the other domain-elements of national power. Attaining cyber power rests on the state's ability to develop the resources to operate in cyberspace. Cyber power as a nation-state capability is no different than land, sea, air, or space power. Instead of tanks, ships, and airplanes, the state needs networked computers, telecommunication infrastructure, programs and software, and people with the requisite skills. As with the land, sea, air, and space domains, the state can produce effects within cyberspace or into another domain through cyberspace.[35] A cyber attack could corrupt an adversary's logistics database, degrading the adversary's rapid deployment capabilities; bring down an air defense network, enabling an air attack; or jam the signals of a global positioning satellite, interfering with a warship's ability to navigate or target its weapons systems.

The U.S. military refers to applications of cyber power as Computer Network Operations (CNO) and subdivides them into three categories: Computer Network Defense (CND), Computer Network Attack (CNA), and Computer Network Exploitation (CNE). These categories are analogous to thinking within China's PLA.[36] The offensive capabilities of cyber power are CNA and CNE. CNA are destructive, "actions taken through the use of computer networks to disrupt, deny, degrade, or destroy information resident in computers and computer networks or the computers and networks themselves."[37] The immediate objective of CNA is to deny the enemy the ability to use their computer systems, stored information, and networks as designed or intended. The secondary objective is to affect all those people, systems, or organizations that rely on that information technology, interfering with or denying them the ability to do their jobs.

CNEs are intrusive, involving unauthorized entry into a network, but do not necessarily cause damage. CNEs are "enabling operations and intelligence collection to gather data from automated information systems or networks."[38] As an enabler, a CNE not only gathers information, but can map networks for future attacks and can leave behind backdoors or malware designed to execute or facilitate an attack. Timothy Thomas, a retired Army intelligence officer and expert on

PRC cyber warfare, believes China's CNEs are reconnaissance missions: mapping networks, collecting intelligence, looking for system vulnerabilities, and planting programs in U.S. networks. This pre-conflict reconnaissance would give the PLA the advantage in a confrontation with the United States. Thomas believes this behavior reflects an old Chinese stratagem: "A victorious army first wins and then seeks battle. A defeated army first battles and then seeks victory."[39]

The distinction between cyber attack and cyber exploitation is both technical and a question of intent.[40] According to U.S. Deputy Secretary of Defense William J. Lynn, "There's no agreed-on definition of what constitutes a cyber attack. It's really a range of things that can happen – from exploitation and exfiltration of data to degradation of networks to destruction of networks or even physical equipment, physical property."[41] Nevertheless, in terms of a nation-state using or reacting to a CNE, the distinction is important. CNE is essentially espionage, historically a common tool for nation-states. International law does not address the legality of peacetime espionage and espionage during armed conflict is lawful under the Hague Conventions.[42]

CNE can also support psychological operations, actions intended to influence the emotions, motives, objective reasoning, and behavior of a specific, targeted audience.[43] According to Richard Clarke, former Special Advisor to the President on Cybersecurity, U.S. cyber units infiltrated the secret Iraqi Defense Ministry intranet prior to the 2003 invasion and sent emails to thousands of military officers. The messages are not public record, but provided instructions on how Iraqi units could surrender without being destroyed. Many Iraqi officers followed the instructions, parking their tanks in rows and sending their troops on leave. The combination of the message, probably a reminder of how the United States destroyed the Iraqi Army in 1991, and the medium, penetration of a secret, closed-loop network, had its intended effect. It convinced Iraqi leaders they would not win and thereby took entire Iraqi divisions out of the war without fighting.[44]

Network attacks and system vulnerabilities might also be introduced through the supply chain. CND is generally focused on preventing external infiltration or attack, but networks can be exploited from within by the hardware and software purchased and installed by the user. A hostile cyber power could access the procurement system and introduce hardware or software equipped with malicious code: back doors for future access, logic bombs to create on demand malfunctions, viruses to infect a network, or kill switches to bring down parts of the network. Deputy Secretary Lynn calls the "risk of compromise in the manufacturing process…very real."[45]

Introduction of corrupted software or hardware would not be difficult given the large number of subcontractors and vendors who contribute components to end item servers, routers, switches and computers. The co-opting of a single employee in the production line could be enough to tamper with significant components – easier still if the cyber power state has industries that export computer network hardware. Software design, conducted by teams of code writers, could be infiltrated even more easily. Or pirated software, reengineered and inserted into the procurement chain, could carry malicious code into targeted networks.[46]

As with the term 'cyberspace,' the terms 'cyber war' and 'cyber warfare' are widely used without common definition. The U.S. Department of Defense defines cyberspace operations as "the employment of cyber capabilities where the primary purpose is to achieve military objectives or effects in or through cyberspace."[47] General Keith Alexander, commander of U.S. Cyber Command, stated: "The focus of cyber warfare is on using cyberspace (operating within or through it) to attack personnel, facilities, or equipment with the intent of degrading, neutralizing or destroying enemy combat capability, while protecting our own."[48] Published articles on the subject agree that nation-states with the capacity for cyber power will fight wars in and through cyberspace.

Cyber war consists of two states fighting <u>only</u> in and through cyberspace, using only computers to attack one another's networks. *Cyber warfare* is conducted <u>as part</u> of a larger, traditional war, combined with land, sea, air, space and other elements of national power. Defensively, cyber warriors will attempt to defend their networks from cyber attack. Offensively, the immediate objective in cyber warfare will be to damage or degrade the adversary's information networks and information technology with the ultimate objective of shaping the overall battlespace.[49] As information technology supports and enables all elements of national power, losing the ability to use national IT systems will significantly degrade a cyber-dependent state's ability to coordinate its resources to wage war. Russia's alleged cyber attack on Estonia is an example of what cyber war might look like.[50] Russia's 2008 attack on Georgia illustrates cyber warfare as part of a larger conflict.[51]

With cyberspace as a war fighting domain, cyber attacks can damage a nation's networks and destroy virtual infrastructure, thereby rendering useless the physical infrastructure it enables. In a highly networked nation-state, the list of strategic cyber targets and the possibilities for second- and third-order effects are nearly endless.[52] Attacks on government and military command and control networks could distract and confuse enemy leadership. Attacking transportation and commerce-related networks could impair supply lines and movement of military forces. Attacks on power grids, water and sewage systems, and financial institutions could cause economic and social panic, weakening national cohesion and political will, and further distracting and confusing the government. Attacking media networks could give the attacker the advantage in shaping global perceptions of the conflict.[53] At the operational and tactical levels of war, a network-centric military could lose its ability to command and control its forces; to access its intelligence, surveillance, and reconnaissance capabilities; even the ability to target and fire weapons systems.

If cyber power is the ability of a nation-state to establish control and exert influence within and through cyberspace, then China has demonstrated that it is a strong cyber power. Most recently, in April 2010, China Telecom[54] – a PRC-owned Internet service provider – introduced erroneous network traffic routes into the Internet. In an event lasting only 18 minutes, these instructions propagated across the World Wide Web causing foreign Internet service providers to route 15 percent of the world's Internet traffic through Chinese servers. Affecting 37,000 networks, this re-routing included traffic to and from U.S. government and military sites, including the U.S. Senate, Departments of Defense and Commerce, and others, as well as commercial websites, including Dell, Yahoo!, Microsoft, and IBM.[55]

In its 2010 annual report to Congress, the U.S.-China Economic and Security Review Commission worried that "[t]his level of access could enable surveillance of specific users or sites. It could disrupt a data transaction and prevent a user from establishing a connection with a site. It could even allow a diversion of data to [a destination] that the user did not intend …." Further, that "control over diverted data could possibly allow a telecommunications firm to compromise the integrity of supposedly secure encrypted sessions."[56] While the Commission could not produce definitive evidence that this incident was a deliberate attempt to manipulate foreign Internet traffic, the Commission believes the event demonstrates that China has the ability to do so at will.[57]

For its part, China Telecom denied that it that it was complicit in hijacking Internet traffic.[58] The PRC foreign ministry responded without directly addressing the Commission's allegation: "We advise this so-called commission to stop interfering in China's internal affairs and do more for mutual trust and cooperation between China and the United States."[59] Historically, China has always denied involvement in any and all incidents of cyberspace intrusion attributed to its citizens, companies, or servers.[60]

China: Objectives, Strategy and Cyber Power

What will China's government do with their cyber power? U.S. government and think tank studies suggest that China has three primary national security objectives: sustaining regime survival (rule of the Chinese Communist Party [CCP]), defending national sovereignty and territorial integrity, and establishing China as both a regional and world power. Critical to those objectives are sustaining stable economic and social development, modernizing the military, and preventing Taiwan independence. The CCP must maintain a position of national and international strength to sustain China's security and their legitimacy as China's ruling body.[61]

While China does not routinely publish documents like the United States' *National Security Strategy*, the China's Information Office of the State Council did release *China's National Defense in 2008*, a document which confirms external analysis. The Chinese government sees itself "confronted with long-term, complicated, and diverse security threats and challenges," including the economic, scientific, technological, and military "superiority of the developed countries," "strategic maneuvers and containment from the outside," "disruption and sabotage by separatist(s)," and the forces of "economic and social transition" causing "many new circumstances and new issues in maintaining social stability."[62]

The United States is prominent in China's assessment of threats and challenges, with mistrust dominating the relationship since the creation of the People's Republic in 1949. Politically, survival of the CCP rests on its legitimacy with the Chinese people, embodied by its ability to sustain economic development and prosperity and protect the territorial integrity of China. Any perceived American interference in these two areas can be viewed as a threat to the PRC's national security. Militarily, the U.S. Department of Defense sees China as a near-peer competitor and is deeply concerned over the PLA's Revolution in Military Affairs (RMA),[63] a modernization program with the potential to challenge America's military presence and force projection in the region.[64]

From China's perspective, they are a rising world power and the United States, as the sole superpower, is both the standard for military technological achievement and China's principal adversary for regional dominance.[65] China sees the United States trying to ring and contain it with military bases and alliances. It sees U.S. concerns over human rights, particularly concerning groups the CCP sees as subversive or separatist elements, as a means of destabilizing the regime. And the American relationship with and military support for Taiwan poses a threat to national sovereignty and therefore regime legitimacy.[66]

Economically, the United States and China are interdependent. America is China's main source of modern technology and a major market for exports. China is the second largest holder of U.S. securities and Treasuries, therefore critical to financing the federal deficit.[67] In order to maintain economic and social stability, China projects that its economy must grow by eight percent a year. Some Chinese feel that the United States is actively attempting to stop China's rise as a major economic power. They worry that the United States will deny them access to resources; manipulate concerns over global warming to drive up production costs and impede industrial growth; or come between China and its Asian trading partners.[68] In America, there is concern over Chinese currency manipulation and its effects on the economy; worry that China would block U.S. participation in Asia-

Pacific economic groups; and general unease about China's growing presence in Africa and Latin America.[69]

History weighs heavily on the relationship, going beyond residual Cold War animosity. China and the United States share a sense of national exceptionalism; a sense of uniqueness and entitlement among nations. China's self-perception is deeply influenced by its ancient history and civilization, predating America by thousands of years. As the world's oldest nation-state, the inheritors of the Middle Kingdom, they are highly sensitive to criticism or interference from outsiders. Chinese nationalism, and their drive to develop into a world power, is partly fueled by the national memory of China's victimization and humiliation by Western nations and Japan during the 19th and 20th centuries. The Chinese chafe at thoughts that they are behind or less than any other nation. Nationalistic pride demands that China develop into and be recognized as one of the world's superpowers.[70] Herein is a potentially fatal flaw to the U.S.-PRC relationship. Seeing the world through an exceptionalist lens, with each perceiving its own actions as "uniquely virtuous,"[71] makes it difficult for both America and China to understand and trust one another.

China's National Defense in 2008 spells out the PRC's national military strategy:

> *China pursues a national defense policy which is purely defensive in nature. China places the protection of national sovereignty, security, territorial integrity, safeguarding of the interests of national development, and the interests of the Chinese people above all else. China endeavors to build a fortified national defense and strong military forces compatible with national security and development interests, and enrich the country and strengthen the military while building a moderately prosperous society in all aspects.[72]*

China's defense strategic framework includes four major provisions geared toward transforming their military and defense systems. First is the modernization of national defense and the armed forces through "informationization."[73] This includes a networked military and development of cyber capabilities. Second is the coordination of national defense spending and economic development, with an emphasis on ensuring ample resources for the military and dual-use industries and technology. Third is the reform of national defense and the armed forces. This includes science and technology, procurement, research and development, and manufacturing, again stressing integrated defense and civilian dual-purpose industry. Reform also includes an improved "national defense mobilization system."[74] The fourth provision is "leapfrogging" military science and technology development; that is, bypassing the gradual, developmental path the United States took to build a networked force in order to equal American capabilities by the mid-21st century.[75]

The thinking behind the PRC's efforts to modernize and reform national defense and defense industry dates to 1991. The PLA was thoroughly impressed with America's military performance in the Gulf War, seeing the advantage high technology provided over a less developed military. Subsequent military actions in the Balkans, Afghanistan, and Iraq convinced the Chinese that having a networked military was a critical American advantage. These later conflicts also demonstrated that high technology forces could be countered or stymied asymmetrically, by low or high technological means.[76] Overall, the last 20 years of American military experience spurred and helped shape the PRC's RMA with Chinese characteristics: informationization of the military, development of asymmetric capabilities, and support of the RMA by the technological-industrial base.[77]

One of the first, open-source indications of China's thinking was the 1999 book *Unrestricted Warfare*, authored by two senior PLA colonels, Qiao Liang and Wang Xiangsui. Impressed with American military technological capabilities and concerned about China's ability to catch up, Qiao and Wang looked at developments in technology, warfare, and the effects of globalization. They argued that it was possible for state and non-state actors to fight a technologically superior opponent asymmetrically. Non-war actions, taken off the actual battlefield, may be more important to winning a conflict than military weapons. The title *Unrestricted Warfare* suggests that future warfare employ asymmetric attacks on all elements of national power – economic, political, information, and military – as a means to deter, intimidate, or defeat a militarily superior enemy. Instead of trying to match

American military strength, China could target America's weaknesses, in particular, its reliance on information technology and satellites.[78]

Whether *Unrestricted Warfare* reflected Chinese thinking or inspired it, China has worked steadily towards creating a modern, informationized force, capable of joint network-centric operations and fighting in and through cyberspace. China down-sized its military twice in the 1990s, while mechanizing and informationizing it, creating a flatter organization supported by information technology for command, control, communications, computers, intelligence, surveillance, and reconnaissance (C4ISR). The PLA has revised doctrine, education and training to support a networked, high-technology enabled force.[79] Its goal is to convert from a mass army to a smaller, more capable military which can win "local wars under conditions of informationization;"[80] a force capable of joint operations which can win against a high technology enemy in modern warfare near its national borders – and potentially beyond. Under RMA, with increased emphasis on a communications network linking all services as well as joint training, modernization of equipment, and the acquisition of power projection platforms, the Chinese military is developing a regional defense capability.[81]

The RMA includes strong emphasis on information warfare and information dominance with a goal to establish control of an adversary's information flow, while denying or degrading the enemy's ability to transmit, receive, access or use information.[82] In February 2007, *China National Defense News* defined cyber warfare as a "use of network technology and methods to struggle for an information advantage in the fields of politics, economics, military affairs, and technology," including a "series of actions like network surveillance, network attack, network defense, and network support," with the goal of establishing network control.[83] The PLA developed an approach called Integrated Network Electronic Warfare (INEW) that combines computer network tools and electronic warfare against an adversary's information systems. Under INEW, the PLA would conduct a coordinated combination of computer network and electronic warfare attacks on adversary C4ISR and supporting networks to deny enemy access to information systems used during support combat operations.[84]

To support INEW strategy, the PLA is actively recruiting technical experts to develop and improve cyber warfare capabilities.[85] The PLA has established at least three cyber warfare training centers for selected members of its officer corps: the Communications Command Academy, Wuhan; the Information Engineering University, Zhengzhou; and the National Defense Science and Technology University, Changsha. Course curriculum and officer training includes radar technology and electronic countermeasures, cyber warfare rules and regulations, cyber warfare strategy and tactics, computer virus attacks and counterattacks, and jamming and counter-jamming of communications networks.[86] Between October 1997 and July 2000, the PLA conducted multiple army and military region cyber warfare training exercises, with cyber detachments conducting CND and CNA against one another. Their tactics and techniques included "conducting information reconnaissance, planting information mines, changing network data, releasing information bombs, dumping information garbage, disseminating propaganda, applying information deception, releasing clone information, organizing information defense, and establishing network spy stations."[87]

At the 2003 National People's Congress, the PLA announced it was activating information warfare units equipped to conduct network warfare and incorporating these units in all PLA armies.[88] Given the 1997-2000 training exercises, this announcement may have been belated; other reports indicate that the PLA had computer warfare units in three military regions as early as 2001.[89] In July 2010, the *People's Liberation Army Daily* announced the creation of the PLA's Information Security Base, co-located with the General Staff Department, to improve Chinese cyber security and strengthen cyber infrastructure. China's *Global Times* quoted a General Staff officer who said, "...our army is strengthening its capacity and is developing potential military officers to tackle information-based warfare."[90]

In keeping with Mao's doctrine of The People's War, the mass mobilization of citizens for war, the PRC's cyber warfare strategy includes incorporating already skilled computer network operators into the reserves and militia. As stated in *China's National Defense in 2008*, "Importance has been attached to establishing militia organizations in emerging enterprises and high-tech industries to increase the technology content of the militia force."[91] Given China's growing computer industry, this creates thousands of prospective recruits. Militia cyber warfare units have been established in several cities[92] and these units are trained in a variety of tasks including CNA, CND, psychological warfare, and deception operations. The PLA not only recruits information technology workers and academics, they also establish militia units within civilian telecommunications and IT companies. For example, between 2003 and 2006, the Guangzhou Military Region established four Militia Information Technology battalions in local firms using the companies' personnel, financial resources and equipment.[93] This gave the PLA use of an already skilled work force and the companies' infrastructure: their computers, network connections, and new software applications. Potentially, this militia-industry collusion could give the PLA access to any company doing business with militarized telecommunications or IT firms, through the company networks or through products developed by the company.

Hackers also play a role in The People's War. Major General (retired) Dai Qingmin, formerly director of the PLA Communication Department of the General Staff and responsible for information warfare, believed that information warfare made all Chinese with computer skills a potential "auxiliary information fighting force."[94] How fully Chinese hackers and hacker communities are integrated into the PRC's cyber warfare strategy is unknown. Chinese hackers have attacked Taiwanese, Japanese, and American websites on multiple occasions. As with the Russian denial of service attacks on Estonia and Georgia, the PRC could make use of patriotic 'hacktivists'[95] to support national objectives while maintaining plausible deniability.[96]

There is evidence of collusion between the PLA, Chinese industry, and hackers. The PLA hosts hacking competitions to encourage hackers to develop CNE techniques and software.[97] Some intrusions into U.S. networks were made using software and tools developed by Chinese 'black hat' programmers.[98] Chinese IT companies who support the PLA have hired hackers.[99] The degree to which the PRC can trust or control the hacker community is unknown. While China controls the state's computer networks, hackers tend to be independent.

Their online activism could as easily embarrass the CCP as support its interests. And the CCP worries that hacktivism could be turned against the Party.[100] China's repeated strengthening of its domestic anti-hacking laws indicates CCP concern over its ability to control its hacker population.[101]

The PLA's concept for information dominance includes kinetic strikes against information systems to augment INEW attacks. Space-based information systems are critical for network-centric nations and the PLA is therefore developing counter-space, information warfare weapons systems, including anti-satellite (ASAT) missiles, lasers, microwave systems, direct energy weapons (DEW), jammers and electromagnetic pulse (EMP) weapons.[102] In 2006, China blinded a U.S. optoelectronic reconnaissance satellite using a ground-based anti-satellite laser. In 2007, China tested a kinetic ASAT missile, using it to destroy a non-operational PRC weather satellite. The ASAT test showed that China can destroy low-earth orbit satellites and the DEW capability allows them to incapacitate a satellite's sensors without actually destroying it.[103]

The U.S. military depends on satellites for many critical functions: ground, air, and naval navigation, surveillance and reconnaissance, targeting precision strike weapons, early warning, and communications. Communications extend from the Pentagon to forward-based units and ships as well as logistics and transportation support, at home and abroad. During the 2003 invasion of Iraq, at peak use, the U.S. military sent and received roughly three billion bits per second of information via satellites. America's communications, global positioning, weather, and reconnaissance satellites are a critical part of network-centric warfare.[104] With anti-satellite weapons in play, this reliance on satellites becomes a significant vulnerability.

China's defense policy calls for the "coordinated development of economy and national defense," making "national defense building an organic part of its social and economic development."[105] From the 1950s through the early 1980s, China's defense industry was a wholly-owned government enterprise. The PRC initiated defense industry conversion, selling some of its military industry and allowing private Chinese enterprises to bid for contracts. At first this caused a brain drain, with employees of formerly state-owned industries moving to the private sector. This trend reversed in the early 2000s with heavy government investment in research and development (R&D). By 2008, China was second only to America in R&D investment. This defense industry conversion spurred development of dual-use technologies, creating an integrated system of collaboration between defense, industry, universities, and research institutes. This serves three purposes: self-sufficiency in defense-related industry, improving China's overall military capabilities, and advancing economic development and prosperity.[106] According to the *2010 Report to Congress of the US-China Economic and Security Review Commission,* this approach seems to be working:

> *China's defense industry has benefited from integration with China's rapidly expanding civilian economy and science and technology sector, particularly elements that have access to foreign technology. Progress within individual defense sectors appears to be linked to the relative integration of each into the global production and research and development chain. For example, the shipbuilding and defense electronics sectors, benefiting from China's leading role in producing commercial shipping and information technologies, have witnessed the greatest progress over the last decade.[107]*

Foreign technology acquisition is a key part of China's dual-use industry growth and helps them to "leapfrog development."[108] Foreign technology transfer allows China to skip years of expensive research and development, eroding the advantages foreign companies and militaries possess. The 2010 report to Congress states: "This network of commercial and government-affiliated companies and research institutes often enables the PLA to gain access to sensitive and dual-use technologies or knowledgeable experts under the guise of civilian research and development."[109]

One means for technology transfer is through joint ventures, which China routinely insists on for foreign entry to its markets. With one billion potential customers, European and American companies would rather enter a joint venture than miss an opportunity for profit. Airbus established a joint venture for its A320 aircraft, giving China insight into advanced aeronautics.[110] Joint ventures with U.S. Lucent Technologies and France's Alcatel enabled China to create a domestic fiber optics industry, allowing the PLA to create advanced Command, Control, Communications, Computers and Intelligence (C4I) networks, sensors in sonar arrays, local area networks in warships, and precision guided munitions.[111] China has four defense-related corporations participating in the European Union's Galileo Project, a system of navigation satellites. This will facilitate R&D for its own dual-use satellite program, potentially including precision strike capability and enhanced C4I.[112] Cisco Systems, a major supplier of U.S. government IT equipment, and Microsoft Corporation have each established R&D and manufacturing partnerships with China.[113]

Some of China's foreign technology acquisitions are less overt and less legal. Globally, multiple acts of computer network industrial espionage have originated from China. As with joint venture technology transfers, CNE of government, research, and business networks provides new technology and information without the investment of time and R&D money. In keeping with 'coordinated development of economy and national defense,' CNE benefits both the PLA and the Chinese economy.[114] Terabytes of information were taken during *Titan Rain* and the infiltration of Lockheed Martin's F-35 fighter program.[115] In 2009, Google executives were targeted in a spearfishing attack from China.[116] When the attack was traced back to the server, Google found copies of proprietary information from Google, Adobe, Dow Chemical, Northrop-Grumman and other U.S. companies.[117]

Foreign joint ventures also have potential to enable future CNE and CNA. China has repeatedly reverse-engineered hardware and software acquired from foreign companies in violation of copyrights, patents, and intellectual property rights.[118] This makes ventures between the PRC and companies like Cisco and Microsoft a potential threat to the U.S. government's IT supply chain. After Cisco began manufacturing routers in China, counterfeit Cisco products began appearing in world markets. In 2007, the Federal Bureau of Investigation (FBI) indicted the owners of Syren Technology for selling counterfeit Cisco routers, switches, gigabit interface converters and wide area network (WAN) interface cards procured from Chinese suppliers. Syren's customers included the U.S. Naval Academy, U.S. Naval Air Warfare Center, U.S. Naval Undersea Warfare Center, the U.S. Spangdahelm Air Base, and the General Services Administration. An FBI briefing on the subject called it an "IT subversion/supply chain attack" that could "cause immediate or premature system failure during usage" or allow "access to otherwise secure systems" and "weaken cryptographic systems."[119]

In order to sell products to the Chinese government, in 2003 Microsoft allowed the PRC to look at the fundamental source code for its Windows operating system, something Microsoft had never allowed a customer to do. Further, to ally China's fears that the U.S. government might use Windows to spy on the PRC, Microsoft allowed the Chinese to substitute their own cryptographic software for portions of the MS code, another first for Microsoft.[120] With the source code, China may be able to identify or create vulnerabilities in networks through the Windows operating system. Conversely, their modified version of Windows would make it harder for someone familiar with Windows to hack into their network systems.[121]

In the future, China will have even less trouble acquiring access to advanced information technology. In 2008, the Chinese government announced a new certification process for imported information technology security products. Foreign vendors will have to provide complete details on how their products work to the Certification and Accreditation Administration and the General Administration of Quality Supervision, both PRC-run testing laboratories. Disclosure requirements cover thirteen categories of hardware and software, including encryption algorithms, software source codes, secure operating and database systems, and intrusion detection systems. Not only does this information include sensitive and proprietary trade secrets, these details will allow the Chinese to copy hardware and software and create means to circumvent these security systems. After negative reaction from vendor nations, China delayed implementation of the requirements until May 2010 and applies them only to information technology sold to the PRC government – which is the largest IT market in China and primary proponent for economic and military development.[122]

The U.S. military and government use Commercial-Off-The-Shelf (COTS) purchasing, from suppliers like Microsoft and Cisco, for most of the information technology used in administrative and combat systems. This reduces costs and enables interoperability across military services. It also introduces vulnerabilities inherent in the software and hardware into both unclassified and classified computer networks.[123] As the vendors who supply the government increasingly outsource software programming and hardware production to foreign countries, the risk that someone might intentionally introduce a vulnerability grows significantly greater.

China, seeking information dominance, would have serious incentive to use its IT industry to create system vulnerabilities, and may have done so already.[124] In 2007, Taiwan's government claimed that Chinese subcontractors had implanted malware in computer hard drives assembled in Thailand. When connected to the Internet, this malware would transmit information from the computers to Beijing.[125] In 2010, India temporarily banned imported Chinese telecommunications equipment. The Indian government had concerns that the equipment might contain spyware which would allow PRC intelligence agencies to access Indian networks. The ban specifically cited the Chinese IT companies Huawei and ZTE, major suppliers for the PLA, and went into effect shortly after media reports that Chinese hackers had broken into Indian government computer networks.[126]

Recalling the PRC's national objectives – regime survival, national sovereignty and territorial integrity, and world power status – and considering their belief that America intends to contain China, how will China use its cyber power vis-à-vis the United States? Most likely, they will try to deter American involvement in China's vital interests. Again, from *China's National Defense in 2008*:

> *This guideline lays stress on deterring crises and wars. It works for close coordination between military struggle and political, diplomatic, economic, cultural and legal endeavors, strives to foster a favorable security environment, and takes the initiative to prevent and defuse crises, and deter conflicts and wars. It strictly adheres to a position of self-defense, exercises prudence in the use of force, seeks to effectively control war situations, and strives to reduce the risks and costs of war. It calls for the building of a lean and effective deterrent force and the flexible use of different means of deterrence.*[127]

As early as 1996, PLA publications on information warfare (IW) discussed the use of IW for strategic deterrence.[128] In 2007, Major General Li Deyi, Deputy Chair of the Department of Warfare Theory and Strategic Research, PLA Academy of Military Science, stated: "Information deterrence…are new modes of strategic thought and are important new deterrent forces, along with nuclear deterrence, in achieving national strategic objectives."[129] Other Chinese publications have echoed this idea and Western experts see this as a trend.

Brian Mazanec, an SRA International senior intelligence analyst, argues that "China's interest in…cyber warfare begins with deterrence." Mazanec believes the PRC plans to use the threat of cyber power to deter the United States from interfering with China's national objectives, both as a counterforce weapon targeting military networks and for countervalue targeting against civilian infrastructure.[130] James Mulvenon, Director of Defense Group, Incorporated's Center for Intelligence Research and Analysis, concurs. Mulvenon states that the PLA sees computer network attack as the "spearpoint of deterrence," an inexpensive, long-range means to strike the United States, with the added advantage of plausible deniability and limited physical damage.[131] Bryan Krekel, Manager of the Cyber Threat Analysis and Intelligence Team at Northrop-Grumman, also agrees. He states that the Chinese see the non-lethal nature of cyber attacks as a key feature to strategic deterrence, analogous to nuclear deterrence. Krekel maintains that the PLA sees CNA weapons as "bloodless," capable of causing strategic level effects, but creating fewer casualties than kinetic weapons.[132]

The aim of deterrence is to discourage an opponent from starting or continuing a conflict by convincing him that he has more to lose by fighting than by standing down. While there are many variations on deterrence theory, most agree that deterrence requires at least four components. First, a denial or defensive capability, the means to prevent or frustrate an enemy's attack. Second, a punishment or offensive capability, the means to penalize the enemy if he does attack. Third, credibility, the enemy's belief that the actor has offensive and defensive means. Finally, a deterrent declaration, a public statement of intent or demonstration of the ability to use those capabilities.[133]

Cyber deterrence is consistent with China's military strategy and the concept of informationized warfare. The PRC has demonstrated that it has an offensive capability and the infrastructure and internal controls for a credible defense. As to a deterrent declaration, Dr. Abram Shulsky, former Special Assistant to the Under Secretary of Defense for Policy, wrote that "The Chinese concept of deterrence…seems to depend more on the cumulative effect of past actions than on specific threats about the future."[134] If Shulsky is correct, the PRC may consider the many PLA articles on information and cyber warfare, combined with known Chinese network infiltrations and its anti-satellite weapons tests, as ample deterrent declaration and demonstration.[135]

Would China risk a cyber attack on America, given U.S. military capabilities and Sino-American economic interdependence? While the two states have many conflicting interests, Taiwan is one place where the United States and China face the real possibility of military conflict. For the CCP, Taiwan's independence is an issue of national pride and sovereignty, therefore a question of CCP legitimacy and regime survival.[136] Faced to choose between losing Taiwan or suffering a military defeat to the United States in a conventional war, a cyber attack to deter American support for Taiwan might be a viable option for the CCP.

China could conduct operational-level cyber attacks against U.S. forces in the Pacific, to delay or degrade their ability to mobilize and move forces to assist Taiwan. China could also conduct strategic attacks on American government and civilian networks, disrupting civilian command and control or critical infrastructure, to coerce U.S. capitulation.[137] Without causing much lasting physical destruction, the PLA could undermine America's military means and will to support Taiwan. For PRC cyber units, the United States is both a soft target and a target rich environment.

American Cyber Dependency and Cyber Defense

In the United States, cyberspace has become vital in all sectors of society – government, commerce, academia, and private life – serving as the preferred medium for communication and distribution of information. The Internet supports hundreds of billions of dollars of business transactions each year as well as critical infrastructure and services such as the electric power grid, water and sewage systems, health care, law enforcement, and emergency response services. Information technology is an enabler for almost everything the U.S. government does: communication and information sharing; research and development; collaboration with educational institutions and the private sector; command and control of military forces; provisioning, sharing, and storing of intelligence; and logistical, managerial, and administrative support work.[138]

The U.S. military is particularly cyber dependent, relying on a global network of 15,000 local area networks and 7 million computers connected by over 100,000 telecommunication circuits, spread across bases worldwide. These networks store and transmit unclassified, secret, and top secret information enabling everything from administration to combat operations.[139] The U.S. government's computerized and networked infrastructure may give it advantages in knowledge management over opponents and competitors; however, this reliance on cyberspace creates exploitable vulnerabilities. The widespread use of IT and networked computers has evolved into a U.S. strategic center of gravity, with the potential to allow adversaries to gain knowledge of plans, capabilities, and operations; deny or degrade communications; and disrupt civil infrastructure and economy.[140]

While the government operates on internal networks, the connections between those networks ride on the 'backbone' of the civilian Internet. Privately owned telecommunications companies are the Internet service providers. They own and operate most of America's cyber infrastructure – that is, the cables, servers, routers, and switches that connect cyberspace. The same is true for the Supervisory Control and Data Acquisition (SCADA) systems that run America's physical infrastructure: power, water, and communications. SCADA control functions are intranets, but are usually connected to the global Internet. In terms of security and government oversight, America's cyber infrastructure is largely unregulated and unmonitored.[141] President Barrack Obama took note of this in 2009:

> *No single official oversees cybersecurity policy across the federal government, and no single agency has the responsibility or authority*

to match the scope and scale of the challenge. When it comes to cybersecurity, federal agencies have overlapping missions and don't coordinate and communicate nearly as well as they should – with each other or with the private sector.[142]

This is not a new problem. In 1997, the Department of Defense conducted *Eligible Receiver,* a cyber vulnerability exercise wherein a 35 person team from the National Security Agency (NSA) simulated a cyber attack on the United States. Using only hacking tools available on the Internet, in two weeks the NSA team broke into power grids and emergency response systems in nine American cities. They also gained access to 36 Department of Defense (DOD) internal networks, sending fake message traffic which spread confusion and distrust through the chain of command. In 1999, the *Zenith Star* exercise achieved similar results. NSA personnel cracked the SCADA systems controlling electric power to U.S. military bases and then overwhelmed local 911 emergency systems with a denial of service attack. Both exercises demonstrated that a few hackers can turn off power grids, prevent emergency service response, and impede civilian and military command and control.[143]

A systematic cyber attack could significantly damage multiple sectors of the American economy and civil infrastructure. An attack on the banking system could cause economic panic, causing runs on banks and crashing the stock market. An IT security company estimated that a one-day, focused attack on American credit card companies could cost $35 billion. Attacks on the power grid could shut down electricity to cities or whole regions: no lights, no telephone service, and no emergency services. A cyber attack on water systems could make entire cities uninhabitable or open dams causing flooding in areas downriver. The ILOVEYOU virus, launched by a single hacker in May 2000, damaged thousands of computer files costing Americans more than $4 billion.[144] A 2007 report by the U.S. Cyber Consequences Unit projected that a full scale critical infrastructure cyber attack could cost $700 billion.[145]

Infrastructure cyber attacks would interfere with local, state, and federal authorities' ability to respond to the emergency. Their situational awareness would be limited by the lack of power and Internet service.

They would be unable to talk internally or with each other to coordinate response. Under such circumstances, America's ability to respond to a crisis elsewhere in the world would be negligible.[146] General James Cartwright, then Commander of U.S. Strategic Command, stated that China has conducted the kind of computer network reconnaissance and mapping of government and private networks necessary to conduct such attacks and has the ability to cripple critical infrastructure and military command and control.[147]

The U.S. government is aware that America as a whole is vulnerable to cyber exploitation and attack, but response has been slow and inadequate. President Barrack Obama has, perhaps, a personal interest in cyber security. During his presidential campaign, the FBI informed then-Senator Obama that his campaign's computers had been hacked in an intrusion originating from China.[148] In early 2009, the Obama Administration began a review of the Bush Administration's cyber security policies,[149] 90 days later publishing the *Cyberspace Policy Review (CPR)*[150] and a 12-point summary of the still-classified *Comprehensive National Cybersecurity Initiative (CNCI)* begun by the Bush Administration.[151]

The *CPR* addresses a wide range of cyber security concerns in very broad terms: restructuring federal bureaucracy, enhancing public education, coordinating departmental policies and expertise, fostering government-private sector cooperation, building coordinated response capabilities, and working with the international community. The 12-points of *CNCI* are more of the same. Combined, the *CPR* and the *CNCI* are essentially plans for a plan, an outline of the many actions that must be taken to eventually build national cyber security. They emphasize some critical points for cyber defense such as hardening government networks and critical infrastructure as well as securing the national information technology supply chain. But even as a plan for a plan, do they address the need?

Richard Clarke, formerly the Bush Administration's Special Advisor to the President on Cybersecurity, provides a harsh critique: "President Obama's *CNCI* is President Bush's *CNCI*, redux....It added a military Cyber Command, but not a cyber war strategy, not a major policy or program to defend the private sector, nothing to initiate international dialogue on cyber war."[152] A year after the release of *CPR*, the Government Accountability Office (GAO) released a report that seems to concur with Clarke's assessment:

> *...according to the President's Cyberspace Policy Review, the cybersecurity policy official should lead specific near-term international goals and objectives; however, it does not further articulate either the specific supporting activities or time frames in which to accomplish this or other objectives. Officials from the Departments of State and Defense stated that, as called for by the President's Cyberspace Policy Review, an effort is currently under way to develop an international strategy for cyberspace. However, we have not seen any evidence of such activities and, thus, were unable to determine what progress, if any, has been made towards accomplishing this goal. In addition, in March 2010, we reported that the federal government lacked a formal strategy for coordinating outreach to international partners for the purposes of standards setting, law enforcement, and information-sharing. Unless agency and White House officials follow a comprehensive strategy that clearly articulates overarching goals, subordinate objectives, specific activities, performance metrics, and reasonable time frames to achieve results, the Congress and the American public will be ill-equipped to assess how, if at all, federal efforts to address the global aspects of cyberspace ultimately support U.S. national security, economic, and other interests.*[153]

Two federal entities bear principal responsibility for U.S. government cyber security, the DOD's U.S. Cyber Command (CYBERCOM) and the Department of Homeland Security (DHS). CYBERCOM's mission is, "to direct the operations and defense of specified Department of Defense information networks and; prepare to, and when directed, conduct full-spectrum military cyberspace operations in order to enable actions in all domains, ensure U.S./Allied freedom of action in cyberspace and deny the same to our adversaries."[154] CYBERCOM coordinates defense of the military part of the Internet, the '.mil domain,' and conducts offensive computer network operations as ordered. CYBERCOM does not control the DOD's network infrastructure or supply chain. The Defense Information Systems Agency (DISA), a DOD support agency, is responsible for acquisition, operation, control, and maintenance of DOD's information networks and individual services manage their own.[155] CYBERCOM has no authority to defend the government (.gov), or civilian (commonly referred to as the ".com"[156]) domains. While it can provide support to civilian authorities, actively defending the civilian domains would require an order from the President.[157] Deputy Secretary of Defense Lynn states that CYBERCOM will work with other government agencies, citing as evidence the presence of FBI, DHS, intelligence community, and Justice Department liaisons at CYBERCOM's headquarters.[158]

DHS is responsible to lead and coordinate protection, defense and response to cyber threats and vulnerabilities for the Federal Executive Branch networks. 'Coordinate' is the operative word; for the most part, DHS relies on inter-governmental cooperation to effect cyber security. DHS operates the National Cybersecurity and Communications Integration Center (NCCIC), directs the U.S. Computer Emergency Response Team (CERT), and has the authority to establish technical operational standards for .gov networks. However, most government agencies within the federal framework have their own internal networks and operating authorities. As with the DOD's four services, each federal office has responsibility for securing and defending their own networks and information infrastructure.[159]

DHS also has the lead for coordinating efforts to protect the civilian domain. This includes preventing damage before an attack and restoring systems afterwards; the latter if there is a declaration of a federal emergency. DHS is the focal point for federal, state, local and private sector cyber security synchronization and cooperation – which is not the same as actually protecting the .com domain.[160] While admitting that civilian networks are targeted by foreign states, Deputy Secretary of Defense Lynn states that, "The U.S. government has only just begun to broach the larger question of whether it is necessary and appropriate to use national resources, such as the defenses that now guard military networks, to protect civilian infrastructure."[161] In fact, there is no federal agency tasked with defense of the .com domain; those privately owned networks which include Internet service and critical infrastructure.

Private sector industries and enterprises are not without cyber security, but their systems are designed to prevent cyber crime, vice defend against a state-sponsored cyber attack. Companies apply best practice business standards to create the level of security their business requires. From a private sector perspective, security is their responsibility, defense is a government responsibility. DHS can work with the private sector through organizations like the Multi-State Information Sharing and Analysis Centers, but DHS cannot mandate security or conduct active security operations for the private, state, and local sectors.[162]

The federal government works with defense industries to implement additional safeguards, as part of contracted work, but has not mandated requirements for private sector cyber defense.[163] In a speech announcing the updated *CNCI*, President Obama stated that the government would not attempt to regulate cyber security for private companies, opting instead to work through public and private sector partnerships.[164] Nascent partnerships such as the Enduring Security Framework, where executive officers and technology officers for information technology and defense companies meet with DHS and DOD, are the government's primary method for encouraging better national cyber defense.[165]

DHS and DOD have their assigned spheres for defense, which leave vulnerable seams between the .gov and .mil domains, and neither department truly defends the private domains. In 2010, Defense Secretary Gates and DHS Secretary Napolitano signed the *Memorandum of Agreement Regarding Cybersecurity* to improve cooperation. They created a Joint Coordination Element to coordinate and deconflict between DHS and NSA; put an NSA Cryptologic Services Group and a CYBERCOM Support Element at the DHS NCCIC to support the *National Cyber Incident Response Plan;*[166] and sent DHS personnel to work in the NSA Threat Operations Center (NTOC) for coordination and synchronization.[167] Gates and Napolitano see this as a means to "enhance operational coordination and joint program planning," so they can "work together to protect our nation's cyber networks and critical infrastructure," and they, "hope that this would drive more rapid collaboration."[168]

'Hope' is not a strategy for defense. Two years after the *Cyberspace Policy Review*, the government remains fragmented with federal agencies still negotiating over who is responsible and who has authority. Despite DHS and DOD collaboration and appointment of the Presidential Cybersecurity Coordinator,[169] there is still no central authority for governmental or national cyber defense. In addition to DHS and DOD, the Office of Management and Budget – through its Federal Information Security Management Act (FISMA) oversight authority – and the Justice Department – with its cybercrime prevention and investigation duties – each have cyber security roles, capabilities, and authorities. Each federal department and agency retains its own networks, IT budgets, and authorities.[170] Deputy Secretary of Defense Lynn states that, "Given the dominance of offense in cyberspace, U.S. defenses need to be dynamic. Milliseconds can make a difference, so the United States military must respond to attacks as they happen or even before they arrive."[171] But according to the Government Accountability Office, U.S. defenses are anything but 'dynamic':

> *Federal agencies have not demonstrated an ability to coordinate their activities and project clear policies on a consistent basis. Multiple DOD officials stated that relationships among a small number of government officials – rather than a formal interagency mechanism – remain a primary means by which agencies avoid policy conflicts.*[172]

Contrast America's position with that of the PRC. The PRC has worked to create an integrated national cyber strategy, coordinating the actions and infrastructure of government, military, industry and education. They established a centralized PLA Information Security Base, whose stated role is cyber defense, within their General Staff headquarters and in close proximity to the nation's decision makers.[173] China's national networks are much like a national intranet, subdivided for government, commercial/private, and academic uses. The PRC owns the physical infrastructure, directly or in partnership with private enterprise, and controls the national gateways to the global Internet. China also has a well-developed content-filtering system, sometimes called the "Great Cyber Wall of China." In effect, the PRC has the ability to monitor and control information passing in and out of China's networks or shut off the flow of data completely.[174]

The primary purpose of this control is censorship; limiting Chinese citizens' exposure to "bourgeois-liberal" and "anti-socialist ideas."[175] However, combined with intrusion detection monitoring, China's gateways form a first line of government-controlled defense. Where the U.S. government declines to regulate security, the PRC mandates and enforces Internet security measures, to include regulation on hardware and software.[176] China has even developed its own operating system, Kylin, based on the FreeBSD open source system. Used by the PLA, Kylin may be more secure than the Microsoft operating systems used in America. And cyber weapons designed for Linux, UNIX, and Windows-based systems may not work against Kylin.[177]

It seems certain that the PRC has developed a ready-to-use offensive cyber capability and a state-wide defensive structure, two of the key components to a cyber deterrence strategy. In contrast, the United States appears to be at a significant disadvantage, its infrastructure vulnerabilities publicly documented and probably mapped through PLA computer network exploitation. If the People's Republic of China is already a cyber power, able to deter or potentially defeat the United States through cyberspace, what are America's options?

Ways Ahead for American Cyber Security

At the 2009 Black Hat Conference,[178] an information technology and security forum, the conference organizer held a special session with "experienced ethical-hackers, former government officials, current bureaucrats, chief security officers in major corporations, academics and senior IT company officials." They listed five things the Obama Administration should do to secure cyberspace:

1. Put Defense Advanced Research Project Agency (DARPA) back to work on research and development, allowing the government to protect its IT supply chain.

2. Pursue federal cyber security regulation, vice coordination and partnership, to include regulating major Internet service providers.

3. Focus on resilience – recovery from attacks, vice attribution.

4. Protect critical infrastructure: do not allow utility networks to have direct Internet connections.

5. Develop and empower appropriate leadership.[179]

The Black Hat attendees recognized that truly comprehensive cyber security requires significant action. President Obama's revised *CNCI* initiatives contain many of the measures America must take to close the gaps between Chinese capabilities and U.S. vulnerabilities: improved government sector defense, public-private sector involvement, and mass education.[180] However, this list of twelve initiatives is barely a starting point. Its primary flaw: the *CNCI* strategy is too *laissez-faire*. In trying to balance federal leadership with federal intervention, *CNCI* perpetuates network critical vulnerabilities. Americans have been complacent and willing to accept the steady-state condition of technological vulnerability and insecurity. Comprehensive network security and defense requires a stronger federal government effort. The United States needs a dramatic change in national cyber strategy to include federal prioritization of cyber defense, legislated or regulated improvements in government and critical infrastructure network security, bilateral discussions with the People's Republic, and an international effort to regulate cyberspace.

Cyber security and defense must be a matter of national security and national defense. National security includes protecting territorial sovereignty and the preferred method of defense is to fight battles away from American soil.[181] American territory now includes its Internet infrastructure and cyber warfare is fought on, within, and through that infrastructure.[182] As government, critical infrastructure, and emergency services are dependent on the Internet, cyberspace cannot be left to the vagaries of public-private sector cooperation and partnership. Attempting to apply best business practices on a national scale is inadequate to the task. Defense requires a new way of thinking about cyber infrastructure security and an approach similar to the way in which the federal government oversees airport security, but broader in scope. Such action will likely be unpopular, requiring strong will and leadership by the national executive.

Responsibility and authority for national cyber defense should be fixed with one federal agency. The GAO found at least eight federal departments with responsibilities for securing parts of American cyberspace, to include policy-making, standards and procurement, law enforcement, and representing U.S. interests with foreign governments.[183] The United States needs a single office with the overall responsibility for and authority to compel interagency coordination and action.[184] Just as the Office of the Director of National Intelligence (ODNI) was created to oversee and direct implementation of the National Intelligence Program, an Office of National Cybersecurity should be created to oversee and direct all agencies involved in cyber defense.[185] The director should be a Cabinet-level post with authority for government, military, and civil cyber defense. This office would include coordinating authority over all federal offices involved in cyber security, cyber defense, cyber crime, regulation, federal equipment standards and procurement to ensure integrated and coordinated efforts. This would better fulfill the first part of *CNCI* Initiative #1, "manage the Federal Enterprise Network as a single network enterprise."[186] Until the U.S. government's internal organizational challenges are resolved, "the United States will be at a disadvantage in promoting its national interests in the realm of cyberspace."[187]

The first task for the 'Director of National Cybersecurity' would be to harden American cyber defenses. The first step in deterrence is denying adversary access to the network; in terms of his cost-benefit analysis, we should make exploitation efforts too costly.[188] *CNCI* has a start on this with Initiative #2, "Deploy an intrusion detection system of sensors across the Federal enterprise."[189] DHS will employ the EINSTEIN series across federal networks. NSA computer programs, EINSTEIN 2 and EINSTEIN 3, use threat signatures to detect malicious traffic and activity entering and leaving networks. Both systems send automated alerts to the U.S. CERT, for situational awareness and to shorten notification and reaction time.[190] However, this system could be improved by the incorporation of content monitoring. Rather than looking for malicious threat signatures, content monitoring scans Internet traffic for sensitive content, thus preventing exfiltration of classified or sensitive information. By searching for keywords, content monitoring can stop and quarantine unauthorized or unencrypted traffic before it leaves the network.[191] The drawback to both systems is the controversy with advocacy groups concerning the protection of individual rights and privacy.[192]

CNCI Initiative #1 also seeks "Trusted Internet Connections" for the Federal Enterprise Network.[193] Ideally, this would limit the number of gateways through which traffic enters and leaves the total federal network and allow EINSTEIN to more easily monitor for malware. A better method would be to disconnect federal networks from the commercial Internet, creating a federal intranet for all internal government work. Based on duty requirements, many U.S. government offices will still require access to the commercial Internet; however, transfer of data from the Internet to the federal intranet could be limited to specific workstations controlled by systems administrators. While this would inconvenience federal workers, it would negate direct CNE from the Internet to government networks. Work hours lost due to restricted Internet access might actually be recouped by preventing employees from surfing the Internet for personal reasons during work hours.[194]

General Keith Alexander, commander of CYBERCOM and Director, NSA, has proposed creation of a "secure, protected zone,"[195] similar in function to the DOD's Secret Internet Protocol Router Network (SIPRNet), but for unclassified work. *CNCI* Initiative 7, "Increase the security of our classified networks," misses the fact that security breaches are on unclassified networks. General Alexander's secure-but-unclassified network would use the Internet's infrastructure, but without direct connection to the commercial Internet. This would prevent transfer of data between the two, but allow communication between authorized users. Alexander would go beyond defense of the .mil and .gov domains; he would include critical infrastructure – commercial aviation, utilities, and emergency services – as part of this secured zone.[196]

Most of America's critical infrastructure and the information technology systems that run them are privately owned. Their cyber security is geared towards preventing cyber crime, not external exploitation or control of their supervisory control and data acquisition (SCADA) systems. In most cases SCADA networks started as intranets; power companies, for example, linking the computers which control and distribute electricity. As Internet use grew, for convenience and efficiency, these networks were linked to the rest of the company network and hence to the commercial Internet.[197]

These connections make critical infrastructure vulnerable and America's potential adversaries know it. In 2009, a graduate engineering student at China's Dalian University published in an international journal a paper entitled, "Cascade-Based Attack Vulnerability on the U.S. Power Grid." While the author claims the paper was an attempt "to enhance the stability of power grids by exploring potential vulnerabilities,"[198] the collaborative relationship between China's universities and military could make this paper a blueprint for CNE targeting. At the very least, SCADA systems must be disconnected from the Internet. Including critical infrastructure in a federally secured network would allow national utilities to remain linked with greatly reduced vulnerability to CNE.

The same security applied to federal networks and critical infrastructure must be extended to the contracted service and supply chains which support federal and critical information technology. *CNCI* Initiative #11 is to "Develop a multi-pronged approach for global supply chain risk management," but speaks only in terms of "managing risk" and "awareness of threats."[199] During much of the Cold War, the United States developed most of its own computer hardware and software through agencies like DARPA.[200] If the government intends to use the commercial sector for IT, industry security must be federally regulated. Regulations must be created by computer professionals at CYBERCOM and the NCCIC, not by industry lobbyists who help write Congressional legislation. Regulation must cover development and acquisition, to ensure hardware and software is malware-free. Vendors must not only ensure their products are clean, but must ensure their research and development teams operate on secured intranets without direct external access to the Internet. This will help ensure that IT is not only untainted, but that the latest developments in cyber security are not exfiltrated and reverse engineered by potential adversaries.

The biggest step the federal government can take is to secure the Internet's infrastructure. Richard Clarke, former presidential Advisor for Cybersecurity, points out that AT&T, Verizon, Level 3, Qwest, and Sprint are the largest American Internet Service Providers (ISPs), controlling the infrastructure which moves over 90 percent of American Internet traffic. Clarke argues that these 'Tier 1' ISPs could mirror the federal government's use of EINSTEIN by placing deep-packet intrusion scanners where fiber-optic cables enter the United States and where the Tier 1 networks connect to smaller ISPs. Intrusion scanners would search for malware signatures provided by NSA. This system could screen for CNA traffic from foreign countries and for domestic malicious and industrial espionage activity.[201] This would move America closer to the level of security China employs, but without government Internet control or censorship.

CNCI Initiative #8 calls for "Cyber Education," but focuses on skills training.[202] National cyber security requires a broad public education campaign, for the federal workforce, its supporting contractors, and the American people. To create support for stringent cyber defense, the American people must understand the severity of the threat.[203] The government has used public education campaigns before, to change minds, behavior and to build support for government policy. The first faltering effort for cyber education, National Cybersecurity Awareness Month, has been largely ignored for the last seven years.[204] Energizing public support for comprehensive cyber security may require a World War II-scale education campaign clearly explaining that cyber defense is a matter of national security. Americans have embraced information technology and the Internet, but do not understand the inherent threats. Like living with the atomic bomb or the Global War on Terrorism, Americans need to adjust to a security-focused way of interacting with the World Wide Web.[205] Like wearing seatbelts, full body scanners in airports, and not smoking in restaurants, the American people can and will accept some inconvenience and adjust to the requirements for greater cyber security.

Coupled with improved national cyber defense, the United States must directly engage with the People's Republic of China. This critical element, an offensive-defensive strategy, is missing from the Obama Administration's *CNCI*. *CNCI* Initiative #10, "Define and develop enduring deterrence strategies and programs," lacks the offensive capability and intent-to-use statement required for deterrence.[206]

Engagement will not be easy. China's public position is that they are behind the West technologically and more often the victim of CNAs. When connected to a CNE event, the PRC's typical response is to deny any involvement and curtly demand that other states stay out of China's 'internal affairs.'[207] However, if the PRC's strategy is cyber deterrence, they will understand engagement on the basis of Cold War-style mutual deterrence.[208]

Through Cold War confrontation and negotiation, the United States and Soviet Union worked out guidelines for mutual nuclear deterrence. The United States and China must establish a similar appreciation for each others' positions – a code of conduct for cyberspace. The two states need to establish an understanding of how far the other will tolerate network intrusions, what might constitute an act of cyber warfare, and how each might react if cyber redlines are crossed.[209] For 20 years, individuals and organizations within the PLA has published articles on what they could do with cyber power. They may be signaling both capabilities and intent, assuming that similar American articles are a response. To date, the U.S. government has complained but not responded legally, militarily, or economically to China's cyber intrusions. This leaves the Chinese to assume that America will tolerate CNE or that the United States is unwilling or unable to respond. The danger in this ambiguity is that China or America might suffer a serious cyber attack and blame it on the other, prompting a retaliation and subsequent escalation.[210] Opening a constructive dialogue now might avoid a cyber version of the Cuban Missile or Berlin Crisis in the future.[211]

Bi-lateral discussions with China must accompany one of President Obama's other goals, developing internationally accepted norms for behavior in cyberspace.[212] This is a systemic challenge, as the GAO notes: "In general, differences between the laws of nations, sovereignty and privacy issues, varying degrees of national technical capacity, and differing interpretation of laws will impede efforts to establish common, international standards for prohibiting, investigating, and punishing cybercrime."[213] For 10 years, the United Nations has tried and failed to enact an international treaty on cyber crime. The latest attempt, April 2010, broke down over normative differences on national sovereignty and human rights. Russia and China wanted tighter government Internet controls, which Western states saw as censorship. The United States and Europe wanted greater authorities for investigation and law enforcement, whereas Russia and China do not want foreign investigators within their jurisdictions.[214]

Norms can be established where treaty partners can be found. The United States is one signatory member of the only international cyberspace treaty, the Council of Europe's *Convention on Cybercrime*, in force since 2004. The Convention has 47 members and includes 10 non-European states.[215] The European Council has lobbied for the UN to adopt the Convention as a global standard, however, China and Russia oppose it and some developing nations see it as written by and for developed nations. While the Convention focuses on crime – financial and identity theft, child pornography, and intellectual property – and not cyber warfare, it forms a basis from which like-minded nations can act.[216] And, as other nations join the Convention, it forms an enforceable norm for the international community writ large.

The North Atlantic Treaty Organization (NATO) is another venue the United States should engage. The denial of service attack on Estonia, which completely shut down its ability to conduct Internet banking and commerce, was ultimately treated as a cyber crime, not an attack on a NATO state. Estonia's Defense Minister initially compared the DDoS to a blockade of national sea ports, an act of aggression under UN General Assembly Resolution 3314.[217] However, Article 41 of the UN Charter says, in effect, that interruption of economic relations and communications is a "measure not involving armed force."[218]

According to CYBERCOM's commander, General Alexander, "there is no international consensus on a precise definition of a use of force, in or out of cyberspace."[219] Left unaddressed, the attack on Estonia highlights the network vulnerability of NATO nations and an exploitable seam in the Alliance's defense structure. If the Alliance is to remain relevant in the 21st century, it must decide how to respond to CNE and CNA.[220] NATO must determine what cyber activities constitute the equivalent of an armed attack, expressed in terms of the attack's effects rather than on the cyber weapons used. Having established a norm, NATO can coordinate response strategy. The NATO norm might someday be the basis for new international laws of war, but in the immediate future, they would set a threshold for NATO's adversaries. Even if not binding under international law, they would serve as a redline to help restrain adversary cyber activities.

The United States should also look to India as a cyber security partner. India is a growing Asian power and a regional rival with China. The two are in dispute over the Kashmir and the Arunachal Pradesh; each is concerned over the others' military power projection capabilities; and India has been the subject of PRC-based CNE. There is already a basis to negotiate cyberspace norms. The Indo-U.S. Cyber Security Forum was established in 2002 for critical infrastructure protection and at the 2006 session of the U.S.-India Joint Working Group on Counterterrorism the two agreed to continue bilateral cooperation on several areas, including cyber security. While cooperation between the United States and India would heighten PRC qualms, it would also force them to take more seriously both nations' stated concerns about Chinese CNE.[221]

In April 2010, General Alexander advised the U.S. Senate, "We must establish partnerships with nation-states that share common goals for lawful behavior in cyberspace. Such agreements would establish expectations of normative behavior for cyber activities and thresholds for bad behaviors that would not be allowed to continue."[222] In the absence of common international norms for cyberspace activities, the United States must work to build multilateral norms that can expand. There is a growing understanding in the international community that cyber threats can be like a pandemic. Computer viruses can spread internationally in hours with the potential to wreck havoc on IT systems in every country. Such common threats form a basis for cooperation.

In designing international cyber agreements and norms, the United States should try to incorporate relevant facets of China's Internet laws. This would make the new norms more applicable to developing nations and make it easier for China to accept them.[223] As more states come together in treaties like the *European Convention on Cybercrime*, China and other non-participating states will increasingly be expected to abide by the growing body of norms and more anxious to be involved, lest they be left out of normative decision-making.

Living and Dealing with China's Cyber Power

The United States was the world's only atomic superpower until the Soviet Union exploded their atomic bomb in 1949. America accepted the Soviets as a co-superpower, developing alliances, policies, treaties, and military forces to mitigate the nuclear threat. In much the same way, America must recognize that its superpower status is challenged by the People's Republic of China's cyber power. In addition, the United States must recognize that, just as the Soviet Union and the United States never fought a nuclear war, China's possession of a robust cyber capability does not mean that cyber war is inevitable.

During a state visit to China, President Obama stated: "Our relationship has not been without disagreement and difficulty. But the notion that we must be adversaries is not predestined."[224] The United States and China are not engaged in a Cold War to determine which political-economic system will govern the world. The Cold War-era China has morphed into a new, hybrid state, still controlled by the Chinese Communist Party, but largely mercantilistic in its domestic and foreign policy. The CCP sees success in terms of economic growth, not military or political conquest. The two states are competitors for economic and political power, but not any more than any other states competing for world markets and domestic prosperity. And if China is building a modern military, complete with cyber warfare capabilities, so is the United States. As the Secretary of State's International Security Advisory Board put it, "while China is preparing for an armed conflict with the United States by seeking military advantages in asymmetric areas of warfare, it appears that Beijing does not want such a conflict."[225]

This is not to suggest that the United States and China could not go to war. Taiwan's potential independence is the most likely reason for a Sino-American military conflict. China's cyber power could be a great force multiplier for the People's Liberation Army in a war over Taiwan, asymmetrically reducing the U.S. advantage at the tactical and operational levels of war while causing economic damage and interfering with American command and control at the strategic level.[226] That possibility aside, the most common cause for war is competition for natural resources. With two of the world's largest economies at stake, China and America might fight over access to oil or rare earth minerals. The possibility of war nearly always exists. Like the Soviets' nuclear arsenal, China's possession of cyber weapons does not increase the possibility of war, rather, its cyber power is a factor to be considered and mitigated.

However, the PRC's demonstrated capabilities for computer network exploitation have underscored America's vulnerability to cyber attack, from China, or another state with similar capabilities, or a non-state actor. As the cyber attacks on Georgia and Estonia and the Stuxnet virus infection of Iran's Bushehr nuclear reactor have demonstrated, China is not the only cyber power in the world.[227] Botnets, hacker tools, worms and viruses, Trojans, and malware of other types are readily available throughout the Internet.[228] Given the total threat, America's current cyber security posture is untenable, with national networks and critical infrastructure vulnerable to attack; the agencies responsible for defense divided and disorganized; and the international community at odds over cyberspace norms and rules.

Just as the Chinese used American military capabilities as their benchmark for their Revolution in Military Affairs, the United States must use China's computer network exploitation capabilities as a minimum standard for developing integrated cyber policy, security and defense. Ensuring national cyber security will not be easy or inexpensive, however, deterring the Soviet Union through 45 years of Cold War wasn't trouble-free or cheap either. As it committed itself to nuclear deterrence, the United States must commit itself to endure as one of the world's leading cyber powers with the capacity to deter or defeat its adversaries in and through cyberspace.

Endnotes

1. Wei Jincheng "Information War: A New Form of People's War," Military Forum column, *Liberation Army Daily*, June 25, 1996, http://www.fas.org/irp/world/china/docs/iw_wei.htm (accessed October 8, 2010).

2. Robert M. Gates, *National Defense Strategy 2008* (Washington DC: Department of Defense, June 2008), 3-5; U.S. Department of the Army, *Operations*, Field Manual 3-0 (Washington DC: U.S. Department of the Army, February 27, 2008), 1-1 thru 1-4.

3. James Adams, "Virtual Defense," *Foreign Affairs* 80, no. 3 (May-June 2001), 98-112 in ProQuest (accessed September 15, 2010); Charles Billo and Welton Chang, *Cyber Warfare: An Analysis of the Means and Motivations of Selected Nation States* (Hanover, New Hampshire: Dartmouth College, 2004), 19.

4. Robert A. Miller and Daniel T. Kuehl, "Cyberspace and the 'First Battle' in 21st -century War," *Defense Horizons* no. 68 (September 2009), 2.

5. Brian M. Mazanec, "The Art of (Cyber) War," *Journal of International Security Affairs* no. 16 (Spring 2009), 6-9, http://www.securityaffairs.org/issues/2009/16/mazanec.php (accessed September 15, 2010); Timothy L. Thomas, *The Dragon's Quantum Leap: Transforming from a Mechanized to an Informatized Force* (Fort Leavenworth, Kansas: Foreign Military Studies Office, 2009), 174-176.

6. Lincoln University of the Commonwealth of Pennsylvania "Internet History," *Connected: An Internet Encyclopedia*, http://www.lincoln.edu/math/rmyrick/ComputerNetworks/Inet Reference/57.htm (accessed November 27, 2010).

7. Robert Hobbes' Zakon, *Hobbes' Internet Timeline 10*, http://www.zakon.org/robert/Internet/timeline/ (accessed November 27, 2010).

8. Internet World Stats, *United States of America Internet Usage and Broadband Usage Report*, http://www.Internetworldstats.com/am/us.htm (accessed November 27, 2010).

9. Ibid.

10. James Jay Carafano and Eric Sayers, "Building Cyber Security Leadership for the 21st Century," *Backgrounder* no. 2218 (December 16, 2008), http://www.carlisle.army.mil/DIME/documents/bg_2218%5B1%5D.pdf. (accessed November 15, 2010).

11. The word "attack" is widely and commonly used, particularly in the media and by politicians, to describe any attempt to access a computer or computer network without the permission of the computer system's owner. In U.S. military doctrine, there are essentially two types of unauthorized access, an attack on or an exploitation of the computer system. A Computer Network Attack, or CNA, will "disrupt, deny, degrade, or destroy information resident in

computers and computer networks, or the computers and networks themselves." The purpose of a CNA is to deny the owner of the attacked system the use of the system or the information stored in or transmitted by the system. Hacking into a computer system to deface a website is an example of an attack. In contrast, hacking the same system to steal information resident in the network is what U.S. military doctrine considers a Computer Network Exploitation or CNE. CNE are "Enabling operations and intelligence collection to gather data from target or adversary automated information systems or networks." The purpose of a CNE is to collect information, not damage the system. CNE can be considered theft or espionage, depending on the identities of the exploiter and the owner of the exploited computer system. See Dennis M. Murphy, ed., *Information Operations Primer* (Carlisle, Pennsylvania: U.S. Army War College, 2010), 169.

12.   James R. Langevin, Michael T. McCaul, and Harry Raduege, *Cybersecurity Two Years Later: A Report of the CSIS Commission on Cybersecurity for the 44th Presidency* (Washington DC: Center for Strategic and International Studies, January 2011), 2-3; U.S. Government Accountability Office, *Cybercrime: Public and Private Entities Face Challenges in Addressing Cyber Threats* (Washington, DC: U.S. Government Accountability Office, June 2007), 4-9.

13.   Billo and Chang, *Cyber Warfare: An Analysis of the Means and Motivations of Selected Nation States*, 14-15.

14.   A distributed denial-of-service attack (DDoS) overloads a network or computer with a massive volume of incoming signals. When the network attempts to respond to the increase in Internet traffic, it uses up the resources (e.g., bandwidth, disk space, or processor time) it needs to operate. The network loses its ability to send or receive message traffic. In effect, DDoS blocks Internet traffic between the target and other networks so that they can no longer communicate. DDoS is normally an attempt to prevent an Internet site or service from functioning efficiently or from functioning at all. DDoS attackers use a network of computers to create this flood of internet traffic. The attackers install programs that allow them remote control of other people's computers. The attackers use self-propagating programs which automatically find vulnerable computers (e.g., those with poor security or weak anti-virus software), attack them, and install the DDoS programs. Those newly compromised computers look for other vulnerable computers. Self-propagation allows a large attack network to be built very quickly. Once an attack network is built, the intruder can order the networked computers to conduct the DDoS attack. See Larry Rogers, "What is a Distributed Denial of Service (DDoS) Attack and What Can I Do About It?" *Software Engineering Institute*, Carnegie Mellon, http://www.cert.org/ homeusers/ddos.html (accessed January 17, 2010).

15.   Joseph S. Nye, Jr., *Cyber Power* (Cambridge, Massachusetts: Harvard Kennedy School, May 2010), 3-7; Miller and Kuehl, "Cyberspace and the "First Battle" in 21st-century War," 2-3.

16. "Project Grey Goose, an organization of 100 volunteer U.S. security experts from government and the private sector, conducted a comprehensive investigation into the cyber attacks. Grey Goose investigator Jeff Carr stressed that 'the level of advance preparation and reconnaissance strongly suggests that Russian hackers were primed for the assault by officials within the Russian government.' While Grey Goose members did not find a direct link between Russian government officials and the hackers, they claim it is unreasonable to assume that no such connection existed." See Stephen W. Korns and Joshua E. Kastenberg, "Georgia's Cyber Left Hook," *Parameters*, vol. 38, no. 4 (Winter 2008-2009): 66, in ProQuest (accessed November 28, 2010).

17. Social engineering is a way for unauthorized persons to gain access to a computer or network. It relies on weaknesses in physical security rather than software, exploiting people's ignorance of proper information technology security. The purpose of a social engineering email is usually to secretly install spyware or other malicious software on the targeted person's computer or to trick the targeted person into handing over passwords or other sensitive information. Former computer criminal and now security consultant Kevin Mitnick popularized the term 'social engineering.' See Microsoft Corporation, *Microsoft Online Safety: What is social engineering?*, http://www.microsoft.com/protect/terms/socialengineering.aspx (accessed January 17, 2011).

18. Bryan Krekel, *Capability of the People's Republic of China to Conduct Cyber Warfare and Computer Network Exploitation* (McLean, Virginia: Northrop-Grumman, October 9, 2009), 67-70.

19. A Trojan horse, or Trojan, is a program in which malicious or harmful code is hidden inside another program or data. The computer user is tricked into installing what he thinks is benign software. Once a Trojan horse has been installed on a target computer system, it activates and can damage software, stored data, or may allow a hacker remote access to the computer system. The term comes from Greek mythology about the Trojan War: the Greeks presented the citizens of Troy with a large wooden horse in which they had secretly hidden their warriors. During the night, the warriors emerged from the wooden horse and overran the city. From SearchSecurity.com, *Trojan Horse*, November 3, 2010, http://securitymanagement.searchsecurity.com/security/kw;Trojan+horse/contentGuide.htm (accessed January 17, 2010).

20. A byte is the basic unit of information in computer storage and processing. A byte consists of 8 adjacent binary digits (bits), each of which consists of a 0 or 1. The string of bits making up a byte is processed as a unit by a computer; bytes are the smallest operable units of storage in computer technology. A byte can represent the equivalent of a single character, such as the letter B, a comma, or a percentage sign; or it can represent a number from 0 to 255. A terrabyte is equal to 1,099,511,627,776 bytes. See Encyclopædia Britannica, *Byte*, http://www.britannica.com/EBchecked/topic/87112/byte (accessed January 17, 2011).

21. Christopher Burgess, "Nation States' Espionage and Counterespionage: An Overview of the 2007 Global Economic Espionage Landscape," *CSO Online*, April 21, 2008, http://www.csoonline.com/article/337713/nation-states-espionage -and-counterespionage (accessed October 25, 2010).

"The so-called "Trojan" espionage programs were concealed in Microsoft Word documents and PowerPoint files which infected IT installations when opened, SPIEGEL reported. Information was taken from German computers in this way on a daily basis by hackers based in the north-western province of Lanzhou, Canton province and Beijing. German officials believe the hackers were being directed by the People's Liberation Army and that the programs were redirected via computers in South Korea to disguise their origin." See Der Spiegel, "Merkel's China Visit Marred by Hacking Allegations," *Spiegel Online International*, August 27, 2007, http://www. spiegel.de/international/ world/0,1518,502169,00.html (accessed October 25, 2010).

22. The Security Service (MI5) is responsible for protecting the United Kingdom against threats to national security. "The function of the Service shall be the protection of national security and, in particular, its protection against threats from espionage, terrorism and sabotage, from the activities of agents of foreign powers and from actions intended to overthrow or undermine parliamentary democracy by political, industrial or violent means. It shall also be the function of the Service to safeguard the economic well-being of the United Kingdom against threats posed by the actions or intentions of persons outside the British Islands." See *Security Service Act 1989*, The National Archives of the United Kingdom, http://www.legislation.gov.uk/ukpga/1989/5/section/1 (accessed January 17, 2010).

23. Rhys Blakely, et al, "MI5 Alert on China's Cyberspace Spy Threat," *The Times*, December 1, 2007, http://business.timesonline.co.uk/tol/business/industry sectors/technology/article2980250.ece (accessed October 25, 2010).

24. Three of the control servers were in the Chinese provinces of Hainan, Guangdong and Sichuan. The fourth control server was discovered at a web-hosting company based in southern California. John Markoff, "Vast Spy System Loots Computers in 103 Countries," *New York Times*, March 29, 2009, http:// www.nytimes.com/2009/03/29/technology/29spy.html (accessed October 20, 2010).

25. Sandia Laboratories is a government-owned/contractor operated (GOCO) facility. Sandia Corporation, a Lockheed Martin company, manages Sandia Laboratories for the U.S. Department of Energy's National Nuclear Security Administration. See Sandia National Laboratories, *About Sandia*, http://www. sandia.gov/about/index.html.

26. Josh Rogin, "The Top 10 Chinese Cyber Attacks (that we know of)," *Foreign Policy*, January 22, 2010, http://thecable.foreignpolicy.com/posts/2010/01/22/ the_top_10_chinese_cyber_attacks_that_we_know_of (accessed October 20, 2010).

27. Frank Wolf, *Press Release: Wolf Reveals House Computers Compromised by Outside Source*, June 11, 2008, http://wolf.house.gov/index.cfm?sectionid=34&parenti d=6&sectiontree=6,34&itemid=1174 (accessed October 20, 2010).

28. Gregg Keizer, "Chinese Hackers Hit Commerce Department," *Information Week*, October 6, 2006, http://www.informationweek.com/news/security/government /showArticle.jhtml?article ID=193105227 (accessed October 20, 2010).

29. The primary means to identify computers used in cyber warfare is the IP address. An IP address is a numerical identification that network management assigns to devices participating in a computer network utilizing the Internet Protocol (TCP/IP) for communication between nodes. In essence, each computer has its own unique IP address, which may be static (permanent) or dynamic (temporary), depending on the network configuration. See Jason Fritz, "How China Will Use Cyber Warfare to Leapfrog in Military Competitiveness," *Culture Mandala* vol. 8, no. 1 (October 2008): 49-50.

30. Siobhan Gorman, et al, "Computer Spies Breach Fighter-Jet Project," *The Wall Street Journal*, April 21, 2009, http://online.wsj.com/article/SB12402 7491029837401.html (accessed October 20, 2010).

31. Dan Kuehl, "From Cyberspace to Cyberpower: Defining the Problem," http:// www.carlisle.army.mil/DIME/documents/Cyber%20Chapter%20Kuehl%20 Final.doc (accessed November 8, 2010).

32. Melissa Hathaway, *National Strategy to Secure Cyberspace* (Washington DC: The White House, May 2009), http://www.whitehouse.gov/assets/documents/ Cyberspace_Policy_Review_ final.pdf (accessed October 20, 2010).

33. Chairman of the Joint Chiefs of Staff, *The National Military Strategy for Cyberspace Operations* (Washington, D.C.: Department of Defense, November 2006), http://www.carlisle.army.mil/dime/CyberSpace.cfm (accessed October 25, 2010); David M. Hollis, "USCYBERCOM: The Need for a Combatant Command versus a Subunified Command," *Joint Force Quarterly*, no. 58 (3rd Quarter, 2010): 48-51.

34. Kuehl, "From Cyberspace to Cyberpower: Defining the Problem"; Nye, *Cyber Power*, 3-7.

35. Ibid; Ibid.

36. "The word cyber does not enjoy widespread use in China, which instead generally uses the word informationization. In 2005, the Chinese military translated its own publication, *The Science of Military Strategy*, into English. Translators added a section to the book entitled 'Selected Chinese-English Terms,' in which the Chinese work for information attack had the alternate translation cyber attack. The Chinese word for informationization had next to it the alternate translation cyberization. Two other related Chinese words were expressed in English as age of cyber information and cyber war. In February 2007, China National Defense News defined cyber warfare as a "struggle between opposing sides making use of network technology and methods to

struggle for an information advantage in the fields of politics, economics, military affairs, and technology." Cyber warfare would be a "series of actions like network surveillance, network attack, network defense, and network support by opposing sides..." See Timothy L. Thomas, "Nation-State Cyber Strategies: Examples from China and Russia," published in *Cyber Power and National Security*, Franklin Kramer, Stuart Starr, and Larry Wentz, eds. (Washington, D.C.: Potomac Books, Incorporated, 2009), 466-467.

37. Dennis M. Murphy, ed., *Information Operations Primer* (Carlisle, Pennsylvania: U.S. Army War College, 2010), 169.

38. Ibid.

39. Timothy L. Thomas, "China's Electronic Long Range Reconnaissance," *Military Review* vol. 88, no. 6 (November-December 2008), 47.

In testimony to the House Permanent Committee on Intelligence, Mr. Peter Kurtz, member of the CSIS Commission on Cybersecurity, made a statement which concurs with Mr. Thomas: "Government networks are being targeted to steal sensitive information and gain understanding of mission-critical dependencies and vulnerabilities." See U.S. Congress, House of Representatives, House Permanent Select Committee on Intelligence, *Paul B. Kurtz: Cyber Security Hearing*, 110th Cong., 2nd sess. (September 19, 2008), 7-9, http://www.fas.org/irp/congress/2008_hr/091808kurtz.pdf (accessed September 15, 2010).

40. William A. Owens, Kenneth W. Dam, and Herbert S. Lin, eds, *Technology, Policy, Law, and Ethics Regarding U.S. Acquisition and Use of Cyberattack Capabilities* (Washington DC: The National Academies Press, 2009), 10-11, http://www.nap.edu/catalog/12651.html (accessed 20 October 2010).

41. Cheryl Pellerin, "Lynn: Cyberspace is the New Domain of Warfare," *American Forces Press Service*, October 18, 2010, http://www.defense.gov/news/newsarticle.aspx?id=61310 (accessed October 25, 2010).]

42. Arie Schaap, "The Development of Cyber Warfare Operations and Analysing Its Use Under International Law," *The Air Force Law Review*, vol. 64 (2009), 139-141.

43. Psychological Operations, also called PSYOP, are planned operations to convey selected information and indicators to foreign audiences to influence their emotions, motives, objective reasoning, and ultimately the behavior of foreign governments, organizations, groups, and individuals. The purpose of psychological operations is to induce or reinforce foreign attitudes and behavior favorable to the originator's objectives. See U.S. Department of Defense, *U.S. Department of Defense Dictionary of Military and Associated Terms*, Joint Publication 1-02 (Washington DC: U.S. Department of Defense, April 12, 2001, As Amended Through 30 September 2010), 376.

On June 21, 2010, Admiral Eric T. Olson, commander of the U.S. Special Operations Command, announced a decision to change the term psychological operations (PSYOP) to "Military Information Support" and "Military Information Support Operations" (MISO). He stated that henceforth the term PSYOP will be eliminated from usage in the military. See Murphy, *Information Operations Primer*, 3-4.

44. Richard Clarke and Robert Knake, *Cyber War: The Next Threat to National Security and What to Do About It* (New York, New York: HarperCollins Publishers, 2010), 9-10.

45. William J Lynn III, "Defending a New Domain," *Foreign Affairs*, vol. 89, no. 5 (September/October 2010): 97-109, in ProQuest (accessed October 15, 2010).

46. Ibid. See also National Security Council, *The Comprehensive National Cybersecurity Initiative* (Washington DC: The White House, May 2009), http://www.whitehouse.gov/cybersecurity/comprehensive-national-cybersecurity-initiative (accessed October 25, 2010).

47. U.S. Department of Defense, *U.S. Department of Defense Dictionary of Military and Associated Terms*, 118.

48. Franklin Kramer, "Cyber Power and National Security: Policy recommendations for a Strategic Framework," in *Cyber Power and National Security*, eds. Franklin Kramer, Stuart Starr and Larry Wentz (Washington DC: Potomac Books, Incorporated, 2009), 14.

49. Billo and Chang, *Cyber Warfare: An Analysis of the Means and Motivations of Selected Nation States*, 8 & 17; Steven A. Hildreth, *Cyberwarfare* (Washington DC: U.S. Library of Congress, Congressional Research Service, June 19, 2001), 12, http://www.fas.org/irp/crs/RL30735.pdf. (accessed October 15, 2010).

50. *Cyber attack on Estonia.* In 2007, the Estonian government authorized the movement of a Soviet-era monument from downtown Tallinn, the national capital, to the Defense Forces cemetery outside the city. In protest to this perceived insult to Russia, 'hacktavists' launched a large scale denial of service attack against Estonian targets including both public sector websites and key infrastructure in the private sector – banks, telecommunications, and media. Websites which normally received 1,000 visits a day were buried under 2,000 hits a second. While it had no direct impact on the Estonian military forces or national security apparatus, the attacks came close to shutting down Estonia's digital infrastructure, clogging government websites, bringing work at Estonia's biggest bank to a halt, and overwhelming the sites of several daily newspapers. While it is commonly held that the Russians were responsible for the attacks, digital forensics could not provide any direct link to the Russian government, which denied any involvement in the attacks. See Miller and Kuehl, "Cyberspace and the 'First Battle' in 21st-century War," 2-3; Mark Landler and John Markoff, "Digital Fears Emerge After Data Siege in Estonia,"

The New York Times, May 29, 2007, http://www.nytimes.com/2007/05/ 29/ technology/29estonia.html (accessed November 26, 2010).

51. *Cyber attack on Georgia.* "In July 2008, South Ossetian rebels conducted a series of missile raids on Georgian villages. The Georgian Army responded by bombing then invading the region. The Russian Army attacked and ejected the Georgians. Even before the Russians attacked on the ground and through the air, Georgia came under a massive cyber attack. Denial of service attacks obstructed traffic into and out of Georgian government websites, shut down Georgian media outlets, and blocked Georgia's access to CNN and BBC websites. As ground fighting began, hackers flooded then seized control of routers supporting traffic to Georgia, the effect being that no Georgian could send email out of the country. When Georgia tried to block net traffic coming from Russia, the attacks were re-routed through China, Canada, Turkey and Estonia. When the Georgian banking sector shut down its servers, attacking botnets sent cyberattacks disguised as Georgian traffic to the international banking system, triggering and automatic shut down of connections to Georgian banks." See Clarke and Knake, *Cyber War: The Next Threat to National Security and What to Do About It*, 17-20.

  The 2007 attack on Estonia was completely cyber in nature. In Georgia, cyber attacks preceded and essentially supported conventional military operation by the Russian military. The cyber attacks prepared the battlefield by causing confusion and denying communication. The Georgian government could not communicate through the internet or voice over internet protocol telephones, therefore the ability to communicate and coordinate government and military response. They lost situational awareness provided by international news services and surveillance capabilities such as GoogleEarth. They lost significant capacity to communicate with other governments or international news about the situation in Georgia. And they lost access to the monetary funds they might have used to defend themselves. See Miller and Kuehl, "Cyberspace and the 'First Battle' in 21st-century War," 1; Eugene Habiger, *Cyberwarfare and Cyberterrorism: The Need for a New U.S. Strategic Approach* (Washington DC: Cyber Secure Institute, February 1, 2010), 15-17.

52. Hollis, "USCYBERCOM: The Need for a Combatant Command versus a Subunified Command," 49-52.

53. Miller and Kuehl, "Cyberspace and the 'First Battle' in 21st-century War," 2.

54. *China Telecom Corporation*: "Formed in 2000 by the Ministry of Information Industry, China Telecom Corporation, Ltd. has…invested steadily in network and service expansion, controlling the largest amount of bandwidth between North America and China and being the first Chinese information services provider to expand into North America through its subsidiary, China Telecom America. China Telecom's reach extends to more than 73 countries, where China Telecom and its global client base enjoy mutually beneficial relationships with the world's most highly-regarded carriers." See China Telecoms America,

About China Telecom Americas: China Telecom Corporation: Key Facts, http://www.ctamericas.com/content.asp?pl=599&contentid=613&id=1&indexid=0 (accessed November 26, 2010).

55. Shaun Waterman, "Internet Traffic Was Routed Via Chinese Servers," *The Washington Times*, November 16, 2010, http://www.washingtontimes.com/news/2010/nov/15/internet-traffic-was-routed-via-chinese-servers/ (accessed November 26, 2010).

56. *2010 Report to Congress of the US-China Economic and Security Review Commission*, 111th Cong., 2nd Sess., November 2010 (Washington DC: U.S. Government Printing Office), 244.

57. Waterman, "Internet Traffic Was Routed Via Chinese Servers."

58. John E Dunn, "Internet hijack claims denied by China Telecom," *Network World*, November 18, 2010, http://www.networkworld.com/news/2010/111810-Internet-hijack-claims-denied-by.html?hpg1=bn (accessed November 26, 2010).

59. Agence France-Presse, "China rejects US Web hijack allegations," *TotalTelecom Online Newsletter*, November 22, 2010, http://www.totaltele.com/view.aspx?ID=460470 (accessed November 26, 2010).

60. Three examples of other instances where the PRC was implicated, and denied involvement, in CNE:

   1. When Chinese infiltration of German ministry networks was exposed on the eve of Chancellor Merkel's visit to China, the Chinese Embassy in Berlin "vehemently denied the report" describing it as "irresponsible speculation without a shred of evidence" – despite the existence of considerable evidence. See *Der Spiegel*, "Merkel's China Visit Marred by Hacking Allegations."

   2. Secretary of State Hillary Clinton's demarche and public demand for a censorship-free internet, following Google's claim that Chinese hackers had infiltrated Gmail accounts owned by human rights activists caused 'concern' in the PRC. China's Vice Minister of Foreign Affairs, He Yafei, responded quickly saying, "The Google case shouldn't be linked to the two governments or bilateral relations....Otherwise it is over-interpreting." See Cecilia Kang, "Hillary Clinton calls for Web freedom, demands China investigate Google attack," *The Washington Post*, January 22, 2010, http://www.washingtonpost.com/wp-dyn/content/article/2010/01/21/AR2010012101699.html (accessed December 8, 2010).

   3. When Canada's Munk Center exposed China's connection to the Ghostnet, the Chinese Foreign Ministry called the allegations "baseless" and stated "that China was opposed to hacking and considered it an international crime." See Indian Express, "China hackers 'stole' missile info, Naxal data," *MSN.news*, July 4, 2010, http://news.in.msn.com/internalsecurity/news/article.aspx?cp-documentid=3771253 (accessed December 8, 2010).

61. Elinor Sloan, *China's Strategic Behaviour* (Calgary, Alberta: Canadian Defense & Foreign Affairs Institute, June 2010), 1-2; Evan S. Medeiros, *China's International Behavior: Activism, Opportunism, and Diversification* (Santa Monica, California: Rand Corporation: 2009), 14-18; James Mulvenon et al., *Chinese Responses to U.S. Military Transformation and Implications for the Department of Defense* (Arlington, Virginia: Rand Corporation, 2006), 7-8; Office of the Secretary of Defense, *Annual Report on Military and Security Developments Involving the People's Republic of China 2010* (Washington DC: U.S. Department of Defense, 2010), 15; Susan V. Lawrence and Thomas Lum, *U.S.-China Relations: Policy Issues* (Washington DC: U.S. Library of Congress, Congressional Research Service, January 12, 2011), 7-9, http://opencrs.com/syndication/recent.xml (accessed on January 21, 2011); Secretary of State's International Security Advisory Board, *Report from the ISAB Task Force: China's Strategic Modernization* (Washington DC: Department of State, October 2008), 1-3, http://www.fas.org/nuke/guide/China/ISAB2008.pdf (accessed October 25, 2010).

62. *China's National Defense in 2008* (Beijing, People's Republic of China: Information Office of the State Council of the People's Republic of China, January 2009), 6-8, http://www.china.org.cn/government/whitepaper/node_7060059.htm (accessed on November 3, 2010); Michael Chambers, "Framing the Problem: China's Threat Environment and International Obligations," in *Right-Sizing the People's Liberation Army: Exploring the Contours of China's Military*, Roy Kamphausen and Andrew Scobell, eds. (Carlisle, Pennsylvania: U.S. Army War College, 2007), 43-50.

63. Western analysts frequently note the difficulty in explaining the relationship between the PLA's 'revolution in military affairs' and repeated Chinese references to defense 'informatization' campaigns. In an effort to resolve these difficulties the U.S. Director of National Intelligence's Open Source Center (OSC) in May 2008 published a short study titled, "PRC Military Terminology: RMA with Chinese Characteristics." According to the OSC authors, "PRC media use the phrase 'Revolution in Military Affairs (RMA) with Chinese characteristics' to describe the process by which China's military and national defense industry is attempting to transform itself into a military capable of winning a limited, local high-tech war. The Chinese concept is built on the Western idea of RMA – the adoption of advanced military concepts and the incorporation of information technology ('informatization') – but also seeks to raise the general modernization level of China's military to a level comparable with those enjoyed by Western militaries even before they adopted the RMA concept." The OSC analysts go on to note, "As in the West, China aims to improve its ability to win a high-tech war by transforming its military through the incorporation of information technology and overhauling its military's organization and doctrine." Chinese authors contend that 'the essence and core of the revolution in military affairs with Chinese characteristics is to bring about the informatization of national defense and army building.' According to the Chinese writers, 'informatization'

involves 'many different elements and aspects, the more crucial of which are the development of weapons and armaments, optimization of the military's structure and organization, and innovations in military theories.' They go on to argue that all these elements have to 'come together to constitute an organic entity.' For the Chinese, 'informatization' appears to be a key element of the revolution in military affairs – modernization of the PLA in a manner intended to realize the synergistic benefits of simultaneous command, control, communications, and intelligence, surveillance and reconnaissance." See Eric C. Anderson and Jeffrey G. Engstrom, "The Revolution in Military Affairs and 'Informatizing,'" *Capabilities off the Chinese People's Liberation Army to Carry Out Military Action in the Event of a Regional Military Conflict*, Prepared for the U.S.-China Economic and Security Review Commission (McLean, Virginia: Science Applications International Corporation, March 2009), 9.

64. Secretary of State's International Security Advisory Board, *Report from the ISAB Task Force: China's Strategic Modernization*, 1-6; Michael G. Mullen, *The National Military Strategy for the United States of America* (Washington DC: Department of Defense, February 8, 2011), 3 & 14; Lawrence and Lum, *U.S.-China Relations: Policy Issues*, 24-25.

65. Fritz, "How China Will Use Cyber Warfare to Leapfrog in Military Competitiveness," 40.

66. Rosemary Foot, "China and the United States: Between Cold and Warm Peace," *Survival* vol. 51, no. 6 (December 2009-January 2010): 134; *China's National Defense in 2008*, 6; Lawrence and Lum, *U.S.-China Relations: Policy Issues*, 1-4, 30-31.

67. Secretary of State's International Security Advisory Board, *Report from the ISAB Task Force: China's Strategic Modernization*, 1-2; Kerry Dumbaugh, *China-U.S. Relations: Current Issues and Implications for U.S. Policy* (Washington DC: U.S. Library of Congress, Congressional Research Service, October 8, 2009), 2-3; Lawrence and Lum, *U.S.-China Relations: Policy Issues*, 9-12.

68. Medeiros, *China's International Behavior: Activism, Opportunism, and Diversification*, 31-35; Foot, "China and the United States: Between Cold and Warm Peace," 134; Chambers, "Framing the Problem: China's Threat Environment and International Obligations," 27-29.

69. Foot, "China and the United States: Between Cold and Warm Peace," 134; Sloan, *China's Strategic Behaviour*, 3-4; Thomas Lum, *U.S.-China Relations: Policy Issues* (Washington DC: U.S. Library of Congress, Congressional Research Service, March 12, 2010), 20; Gary Feuerberg, "Experts Urge Action on Chinese Currency Manipulation," *The Epoch Times*, September 22, 2010, http://www.theepochtimes.com/n2/content/view/43023/ (accessed November 26, 2010).

70. Medeiros, *China's International Behavior: Activism, Opportunism, and Diversification*, 10-11; Foot, "China and the United States: Between Cold and

Warm Peace," 129-130; Zbigniew Brezinkski, *The Geostrategic Triad: Living with China, Europe, and Russia* (Washington DC: Center for Strategic and International Studies, 2001), 8-9; Secretary of State's International Security Advisory Board, *Report from the ISAB Task Force: China's Strategic Modernization,* 2-4.

71. Foot, "China and the United States: Between Cold and Warm Peace," 130.

72. *China's National Defense in 2008,* 7.

73. Ibid.

74. Ibid, 8.

75. Ibid, 8-9.

76. Mazanec, "The Art of (Cyber) War," 1-3; Sloan, *China's Strategic Behaviour,* 4-5.

77. Arthur S. Ding, "China's Revolution in Military Affairs: An Uphill Endeavour," *Security Challenges,* vol. 4 no. 4 (Summer 2008): 81-82; David Finkelstein, "China's National Military Strategy: An Overview of the 'Military Strategic Guidelines,'" in *Right-Sizing the People's Liberation Army: Exploring the Contours of China's Military,* Roy Kamphausen and Andrew Scobell, eds. (Carlisle, Pennsylvania: U.S. Army War College, 2007), 102-103; Larry M. Wortzel, "PLA Command, Control and Targeting Architectures: Theory, Doctrine, and Warfighting Applications," in *Right-Sizing the People's Liberation Army: Exploring the Contours of China's Military,* Roy Kamphausen and Andrew Scobell, eds. (Carlisle, Pennsylvania: U.S. Army War College, 2007), 191-194.

78. Qiao Liang and Wang Xiangsui, *Unrestricted Warfare* (Beijing: PLA Literature and Arts Publishing House, February 1999), 8-12, 25-29, 210-214 & 220-222, http://citeseerx.ist.psu.edu/viewdoc/download?doi=10.1.1.169.7179[1].pdf (accessed on October 18, 2010).

79. Ding, "China's Revolution in Military Affairs: An Uphill Endeavour," 81-83; Thomas, *The Dragon's Quantum Leap: Transforming from a Mechanized to an Informatized Force,* 174-184.

80. *China's National Defense in 2008,* 8.

81. Krekel, *Capability of the People's Republic of China to Conduct Cyber Warfare and Computer Network Exploitation,* 6-7.

82. Ibid.

83. Thomas, "Nation-State Cyber Strategies: Examples from China and Russia," 466.

84. Krekel, *Capability of the People's Republic of China to Conduct Cyber Warfare and Computer Network Exploitation,* 6-7; Office of the Secretary of Defense, *Annual Report on Military and Security Developments Involving the People's Republic of China 2010,* 37.

85. Billo and Chang, *Cyber Warfare: An Analysis of the Means and Motivations of Selected Nation States*, 32-33.

86. Ibid.

87. Ibid.

88. Thomas, *The Dragon's Quantum Leap: Transforming from a Mechanized to an Informatized Force*, 180.

89. Monika Chansoria, "'Informationising' Warfare: China Unleashes the Cyber and Space Domain," *Centre for Land Warfare Studies Manekshaw Paper* no. 20 (New Delhi, India: Knowledge World Publishers, 2010), 15, http://claws.in/download.php?action+1270592252MP-20.pdf (accessed December 8, 2010).

90. Russell Hsiao, "China's Cyber Command?" *China Brief: A Journal of Analysis and Information* vol. 10, no. 15, July 22, 2010, http://www.jamestown.org/uploads/media/cb_010_74.pdf (accessed November 25, 2010); Tania Branigan, "Chinese army to target cyber war threat," *The Guardian*, July 22, 2010, http://www.guardian.co.uk/world/2010/jul/22/chinese-army-cyber-war-department, (accessed November 25, 2010).

91. *China's National Defense in 2008*, 37.

92. Billo and Chang, *Cyber Warfare: An Analysis of the Means and Motivations of Selected Nation States*, 33.

93. Krekel, *Capability of the People's Republic of China to Conduct Cyber Warfare and Computer Network Exploitation*, 33-36.

94. Thomas, "Nation-State Cyber Strategies: Examples from China and Russia," 471.

95. "Hacktivist" is a combination of the words 'hacker' and 'activist,' a slang term for a person who changes or manipulates information on the Internet in order to convey a political message. See Macmillan Dictionary, "Buzzword – hacktivist," http://www.macmillandictionary.com/buzzword/entries/hacktivist.html, (accessed December 8, 2010).

96. Vincent Wei-cheng Wang and Gwendolyn Stamper, "Asymmetric war? Implications for China's information warfare strategies," *American Asian Review*. vol. 20, iss. 4 (Winter 2002), 167-178, in ProQuest (accessed September 15, 2010).

97. Simon Elegant, "Enemies at The Firewall," *Time Magazine*, December 6, 2007, http://www.time.com/time/magazine/article/0,9171,1692063-2,00.html (Accessed November 28, 2010).

98. Krekel, *Capability of the People's Republic of China to Conduct Cyber Warfare and Computer Network Exploitation*, 7-8.

99. Gregg Keizer, "Chinese firm hired Blaster hacking group, says U.S. cable," *ComputerWorld*, December 6, 2010, http://www.computerworld.com/s/article/9199898/Chinese_firm_hired_Blaster_hacking_group_says_U.S._

cable (accessed December 8, 2010); "US embassy cables: China uses access to Microsoft source code to help plot cyber warfare, US fears," *The Guardian*, December 4, 2010, http://www.guardian.co.uk/world/us-embassy-cables-documents/214462 (accessed December 8, 2010).

100. James Mulvenon, "PLA Computer Network Operations: Scenarios, Doctrine, Organizations, and Capability," in *Beyond the Strait: PLA Missions other than Taiwan*, Roy Kamphausen, et al., ed. (Carlisle, Pennsylvania: U.S. Army War College, Strategic Studies Institute: April 2009), 256-257; Nigel Inkster, "China in Cyberspace," *Survival* vol. 52, no. 4 (July 2010), 60, http://www.informaworld.com/smpp/title~content=t713659919 (accessed November 8, 2010)

101. Information Office of the State Council of the People's Republic of China, *White Paper: The Internet in China*, June 8, 2010, http://www.gov.cn/english/2010-06/08/content_1622956_7.htm (accessed November 28, 2010).

102. Krekel, *Capability of the People's Republic of China to Conduct Cyber Warfare and Computer Network Exploitation*, 6-7, 12-13.

103. Office of the Secretary of Defense, *Annual Report to Congress: Military Power of the People's Republic of China 2009*, (Washington DC: U.S. Department of Defense, 2009), 14; Matthew Davis, "Dominating the final frontier," *BBC News*, October 19, 2006, http://news.bbc.co.uk/2/hi/americas/6068304.stm (accessed November 28, 2010); Ehsan Ahrari, "US turns space into its colony," *The Asia Times Online*, October 20, 2006, http://www.atimes.com/atimes/Front_Page/HJ20Aa02.html (accessed November 28, 2010); Anderson and Engstrom, *Capabilities off the Chinese People's Liberation Army to Carry Out Military Action in the Event of a Regional Military Conflict*, 50-51; Dumbaugh, *China-U.S. Relations: Current Issues and Implications for U.S. Policy*, 2-3.

104. Sloan, *China's Strategic Behaviour*, 9-10; Noah Shachtman, "How China Loses the Coming Space War," *Wired.com* - The Danger Room, January 10, 2008, http://www.wired.com/dangerroom/2008/01/inside-the-chin/ (accessed November 28, 2010).

105. *China's National Defense in 2008*, 7-9.

106. Ding, "China's Revolution in Military Affairs: An Uphill Endeavour," 82, 87 & 92.

107. *2010 Report to Congress of the US-China Economic and Security Review Commission*, 43.

108. *China's National Defense in 2008*, 7.

109. *2010 Report to Congress of the US-China Economic and Security Review Commission*, 6.

110. Ibid., 99-100.

111. Ding, "China's Revolution in Military Affairs: An Uphill Endeavour," 96-97.

112. Ibid., 93-95; Fritz, "How China Will Use Cyber Warfare to Leapfrog in Military Competitiveness," 33.

113. Clarke and Knake, *Cyber War: The Next Threat to National Security and What to Do About It*, 94-95; "Major Foreign Companies in China," *China Radio International*, http://english.cri.cn/1702/2004-10-29/116@163189.htm (accessed November 28, 2010).

114. Fritz, "How China Will Use Cyber Warfare to Leapfrog in Military Competitiveness," 57; Krekel, *Capability of the People's Republic of China to Conduct Cyber Warfare and Computer Network Exploitation*, 58.

115. Rogin, "The Top 10 Chinese Cyber Attacks (that we know of)."

116. "Spearfishing" is a social engineering tactic used to introduce malware on to a computer. The hacker sends an email message personalized so as to appeal to specific people in hopes that the targeted person will open the email or an email attachment. Upon opening, the email downloads malware to the targeted person's computer. This is called "spearfishing" because it targets a specific individual or persons, rather than the technique of sending out a broad-based message – or "spamming" – to a large number of people. See Protect My ID.com, "Types of Identity Fraud – Spear Fishing," http://www.protectmyid. com/identity-theft-protection-resources/types-of-fraud/spear-fishing.aspx, (accessed January 17, 2010).

117. *2010 Report to Congress of the US-China Economic and Security Review Commission*, 237-239; Clarke and Knake, *Cyber War: The Next Threat to National Security and What to Do About It*, 60-61.

118. Fritz, "How China Will Use Cyber Warfare to Leapfrog in Military Competitiveness," 41; Lawrence and Lum, *U.S.-China Relations: Policy Issues*, 13; Morrison, *China-U.S. Trade Issues*, 21-23.

119. "FBI: China may use counterfeit Cisco routers to penetrate U.S. networks," *World Tribune*, May 15, 2008, http://www.worldtribune.com/worldtribune/ WTARC/2008/ea_china0141_05_15.asp (accessed November 28, 2010); Clarke and Knake, *Cyber War: The Next Threat to National Security and What to Do About It*, 55-57.

120. David Kirkpatrick, "How Microsoft conquered China - Or is it the other way around?" *Fortune Magazine*, July 17 2007, http://money.cnn.com/magazines/ fortune/fortune_archive/2007/07/23/100134488/ (accessed November 28, 2010).

121. Clarke and Knake, *Cyber War: The Next Threat to National Security and What to Do About It*, 55-57.

122. Kevin Coleman, "China Demands Computer Encryption Codes From Cyber Security Firms," *DefenseTech.org*, May 3, 2010, http://defensetech. org/2010/05/03/china-demands-computer-encryption-codes-from-cyber-security-firms/ (accessed October 29, 2010); Joe McDonald, "China scales

back IT disclosure demands," *Sydney Morning Herald*, April 30, 2009, http://news.smh.com.au/breaking-news-technology/china-scales-back-it-disclosure-demands-20090430-aod1.html (accessed October 29, 2010); *2010 Report to Congress of the US-China Economic and Security Review Commission*, 244-245.

Chinese rules for information technology imports cover the following categories:
1. Firewalls (hardware & software) but it does not apply to personal firewalls
2. Network security separation cards and line selectors
3. Security isolation and information exchange products
4. Secure network routers
5. Chip operating systems (COS)
6. Data backup and recovery products
7. Secure operating systems
8. Secure database systems
9. Anti-spam products
10. Intrusion detection systems
11. Network vulnerability scanning products
12. Security auditing products
13. Web site recovery products

123. Clay Wilson, *Botnets, Cybercrime, and Cyber Terrorism: Vulnerabilities and Policy Issues for Congress* (Washington, DC: U.S. Library of Congress, Congressional Research Service, January 29, 2008), 20.

124. Billo and Chang, *Cyber Warfare: An Analysis of the Means and Motivations of Selected Nation States*, 9-10.

125. Christopher Burgess, "Nation States' Espionage and Counterespionage: An Overview of the 2007 Global Economic Espionage Landscape."

126. Nirmala George, "India Bans Chinese telecom equipment," *The Boston Globe*, April 30, 2010, http://www.boston.com/business/techn...com_equipment/ (accessed September 29, 2010); Krekel, *Capability of the People's Republic of China to Conduct Cyber Warfare and Computer Network Exploitation*, 49-50

127. *China's National Defense in 2008*, 9.

128. James Mulvenon, "The PLA and Information Warfare," in James Mulvenon and Richard H. Yang, ed., *The People's Liberation Army in the Information Age* (Washington DC: RAND, 1999), 182.

129. Chansoria, "'Informationising' Warfare: China Unleashes the Cyber and Space Domain," 5.

130. Mazanec, "The Art of (Cyber) War," 3.

131. Mulvenon, "PLA Computer Network Operations: Scenarios, Doctrine, Organizations, and Capability," 257-259.

132. Krekel, *Capability of the People's Republic of China to Conduct Cyber Warfare and Computer Network Exploitation*, 19-20.

133. Martin C. Libicki, *Cyberdeterrence and Cyberwar* (Arlington, Virginia: Rand Corporation, 2009), 7-8; Richard Kugler, "Deterrence of Cyber Attacks," published in *Cyber Power and National Security*, Franklin Kramer, Stuart Starr, and Larry Wentz, ed. (Washington DC: Potomac Books, Incorporated, 2009), 327; William Goodman, "Cyber Deterrence: Tougher in Theory than in Practice?" *Strategic Studies Quarterly*, vol. 4, no. 3 (Fall 2010), 102-128.

134. Abram N. Shulsky, *Deterrence Theory and Chinese Behavior* (Santa Monica, California: RAND Corporation, 2000), 55.

Dr. Evan Medeiros, a senior political scientist at the RAND Corporation and former External Researcher for the U.S. Army War College Strategic Studies Institute, concurs with Shulsky. "China's most acute concerns about U.S. intentions are seldom directly articulated in official statements, but these themes persist in the writings of scholars and analysts – and across a broad range of issues beyond military ones." See Medeiros, *China's International Behavior: Activism, Opportunism, and Diversification*, 31.

135. Thomas, *The Dragon's Quantum Leap: Transforming from a Mechanized to an Informatized Force*, 187.

136. Lawrence and Lum, *U.S.-China Relations: Policy Issues*, 1-4, 30-31.

137. Mazanec, "The Art of (Cyber) War," 3-5; Krekel, *Capability of the People's Republic of China to Conduct Cyber Warfare and Computer Network Exploitation*, 8.

138. Billo and Chang, *Cyber Warfare: An Analysis of the Means and Motivations of Selected Nation States*, 9-10; U.S. Government Accountability Office, *Cyberspace: United States Faces Challenges in Addressing Global Cybersecurity and Governance* (Washington DC: U.S. Government Accountability Office, July 2010), 2-4.

139. Elihu Zimet and Charles Barry, "Military Service Cyber Overview," published in Larry Wentz, ed, *Military Perspectives on Cyber power* (Washington DC: National Defense University, July 2009), 11; Lynn, "Defending a New Domain," 97-109.

140. Billo and Chang, *Cyber Warfare: An Analysis of the Means and Motivations of Selected Nation States*, 16; U.S. Congress, House of Representatives, House Permanent Select Committee on Intelligence, *Paul B. Kurtz: Cyber Security Hearing*, 2, 7-11.

141. U.S. Government Accountability Office, *Cyberspace: United States Faces Challenges in Addressing Global Cybersecurity and Governance*, 3; Peter D. Gasper, "Cyber Threat to Critical Infrastructure 2010-2015," *The Nexus*, vol. 2/1 (February 24, 2009): 2-3.

142. White House Office of the Press Secretary, "Remarks by the President on Securing our Nation's Cyber Infrastructure," press release, May 29, 2009,

http://www.whitehouse.gov/the_press_office/Remarks-by-the-Presidenton-Securing-Our-Nations-Cyber-Infrastructure/ (accessed October 25, 2010).

143. Adams, "Virtual Defense," 98-112; Hildreth, *Cyberwarfare*, 4-5; Ellen Nakashima, "Warriors in the Battle for Cyberspace," *The Washington Post*, September 24, 2010, A-18.

144. Adams, "Virtual Defense," 98-112.

145. Habiger, *Cyberwarfare and Cyberterrorism: The Need for a New U.S. Strategic Approach*, 15-17.

146. Ibid.

147. U.S. Congress, House of Representatives, Committee on Foreign Affairs, *Larry M. Wortzel: China's Approach to Cyber Operations: Implications for the United States*, 111th Congress, 2nd sess., March 10, 2010, 3-4; Krekel, *Capability of the People's Republic of China to Conduct Cyber Warfare and Computer Network Exploitation*, 51-53.

148. Both the Obama and Senator John McCain campaign teams were targeted by a computer network exploitation originating from China: "The hackers were looking for policy data as a way to predict the positions of the future winner. Senior campaign staffers have acknowledged that the Chinese government contacted one campaign and referred to information that could only have been gained from the theft....In the McCain case, Chinese officials later approached staff members about information that had appeared only in restricted e-mails, according to a person close to the campaign." See Ellen Nakashima and John Pomfret, "China proves to be an aggressive foe in cyberspace," *The Washington Post*, November 11, 2009, http://www.washingtonpost.com/wp-dyn/content/article/2009/11/10/ AR2009111017588.html (accessed October 20, 2010).

149. The George W. Bush administration addressed cybersecurity in three policy documents, *National Strategy to Secure Cyberspace, National Strategy for Homeland Security,* 2003 and 2007, and *National Security Presidential Directive 54/ Homeland Security Presidential Directive 23,* also known as the *Comprehensive National Cybersecurity Initiative (CNCI).* While these documents acknowledged cyberspace threats and their asymmetric nature, they provided little to no. specific guidance on how the United States would prevent cyber attacks. The Bush Administration tended to couch cybersecurity threats and responses in terms of their place and application in the Global War on Terrorism. Each of the documents spoke in broad terms of prevention through denial and deterrence and of deterrence in terms of the right to respond to cyber attack through all instruments of national power. See George W. Bush, *National Strategy to Secure Cyberspace* (Washington DC: The White House, February 2003), 50-51, http://www.us-cert.gov/reading_room/cyberspace_strategy.pdf (accessed October 20, 2010); George W. Bush, *National Strategy for Homeland Security* (Washington DC: The White House, June 2002), http://www.dhs.gov/xlibrary/assets/book.pdf. (accessed October 20, 2010); George W. Bush,

National Strategy for Homeland Security (Washington DC: The White House, October 2007), 25-27, http://www.dhs.gov/xlibrary/assets/book.pdf (accessed October 20, 2010).

150. Melissa Hathaway, *Cyberspace Policy Review: Assuring a Trusted and Resilient Information and Communications Infrastructure* (Washington DC: The White House, May 2009), http://www.whitehouse.gov/assets/documents/Cyberspace_Policy_Review_final.pdf (accessed October 20, 2010).

151. National Security Council, *The Comprehensive national Cybersecurity Initiative.* The twelve *CNCI* initiatives released by the Obama White House:

    1. Manage the Federal Enterprise Network as a single network enterprise with Trusted Internet Connections.

    2. Deploy an intrusion detection system of sensors across the Federal enterprise.

    3. Pursue deployment of intrusion prevention systems across the Federal enterprise.

    4. Coordinate and redirect research and development (R&D) efforts.

    5. Connect current cyber ops centers to enhance situational awareness.

    6. Develop and implement a government-wide cyber counterintelligence (CI) plan.

    7. Increase the security of our classified networks.

    8. Expand cyber education.

    9. Define and develop enduring "leap-ahead" technology, strategies, and programs.

    10. Define and develop enduring deterrence strategies and programs.

    11. Develop a multi-pronged approach for global supply chain risk management.

    12. Define the Federal role for extending cybersecurity into critical infrastructure domains.

152. Clarke and Knake, *Cyber War: The Next Threat to National Security and What to Do About It*, 118-119.

153. U.S. Government Accountability Office, *Cyberspace: United States Faces Challenges in Addressing Global Cybersecurity and Governance*, 32-33.

154. A sub-unified command subordinate to U.S. Strategic Command, CYBERCOM was established in 2009 by combining Joint Functional Component Command-Network Warfare (JFCC-NW) and Joint Task Force – Global Network Operations (JTF-GNO) and the addition of four service cyber commands, Army Forces Cyber Command, the Marine Corps Forces Cyberspace Command, the U.S. Navy's 10th Fleet, and the 24th Air Force. CYBERCOM's commander, General Keith Alexander, also serves as the Director of the National Security Agency (NSA). See U.S. Cyber Command

Public Affairs, *Fact Sheet: U.S. CYBERCOMMAND*, October 2010, http://www.stratcom.mil/factsheets/cc/ (accessed October 15, 2010).

155. U.S. Congress, Senate, Senate Armed Services Committee, *Advance Questions for Lieutenant General Keith Alexander, USA, Nominee for Commander, United States Cyber Command*, 111th Congress, 2nd session, April 14 & 15, 2010, 26, http://armed-services.senate.gov/statemnt/2010/.../Alexander%2004-15-10.pdf (accessed October 27, 2010).

156. Most Americans use the term ".com" (pronounced "dot com") to refer to the commercial and private sector owned and operated part of the internet. In fact, .com includes only part of the civilian internet infrastructure. In the Domain Name System (DNS) there is a hierarchy of names for non-governmental computer addresses including .com, .net, .org, and .edu. See Postel, below. This paper uses the term ".com" in its colloquial sense, referring to the non-federal government portions of the American internet structure. A more technical explanation follows from Jonathan Bruce Postel, Internet Engineering Task Force (IETF), "Memorandum: Domain Name System Structure and Delegation" (March 1994), http://www.ietf.org/rfc/rfc1591.txt (accessed on January 21, 2011).

"In the Domain Name System (DNS) naming of computers there is a hierarchy of names. The root of system is unnamed. There are a set of what are called "top-level domain names" (TLDs). These are the generic TLDs (EDU, COM, NET, ORG, GOV, MIL, and INT), and the two letter country codes. Each of the generic TLDs was created for a general category of organizations. The country code domains (for example, FR, NL, KR, US) are each organized by an administrator for that country. These administrators may further delegate the management of portions of the naming tree. Of these generic domains, five are international in nature, and two are restricted to use by entities in the United States.

World Wide Generic Domains:

COM: This domain is intended for commercial entities, that is companies. This domain has grown very large and there is concern about the administrative load and system performance if the current growth pattern is continued. Consideration is being taken to subdivide the COM domain and only allow future commercial registrations in the subdomains.

EDU: This domain was originally intended for all educational institutions. Many Universities, colleges, schools, educational service organizations, and educational consortia have registered here.

NET: This domain is intended to hold only the computers of network providers, that is the NIC and NOC computers, the administrative computers, and the network node computers.

ORG: This domain is intended as the miscellaneous TLD for organizations that didn't fit anywhere else. Some non-government organizations may fit here.

INT: This domain is for organizations established by international treaties, or international databases.

United States Only Generic Domains:

GOV: This domain was originally intended for any kind of government office or agency. More recently a decision was taken to register only agencies of the U.S. Federal government in this domain. State and local agencies are registered in the country domains.

MIL: This domain is used by the U.S. military.

Example country code Domain:

US: As an example of a country domain, the US domain provides for the registration of all kinds of entities in the United States on the basis of political geography, that is, a hierarchy of <entity-name>.<locality>.<state-code>.US. For example, "IBM.Armonk.NY.US." In addition, branches of the US domain are provided within each state for schools (K12), community colleges (CC), technical schools (TEC), state government agencies (STATE), councils of governments (COG), libraries (LIB), museums (MUS), and several other generic types of entities."

157. U.S. Congress, Senate, Senate Armed Services Committee, *Advance Questions for Lieutenant General Keith Alexander, USA, Nominee for Commander, United States Cyber Command*, 3-4, 12.

158. Lynn, "Defending a New Domain," 97-109.

159. Department of Homeland Security, *White Paper: Computer Network Security & Privacy Protection*, February 19, 2010, http://www.dhs.gov/files/publications/editorial_0514.shtm#4 (accessed October 27, 2010).

160. Ibid; Clarke and Knake, *Cyber War: The Next Threat to National Security and What to Do About It*, 121-122.

161. Lynn, "Defending a New Domain," 97-109.

162. Clarke and Knake, *Cyber War: The Next Threat to National Security and What to Do About It*, 119-122, 143-144; Inkster, "China in Cyberspace," 65; James R. Langevin, Michael T. McCaul, and Harry Raduege, *Cybersecurity Two Years Later: A Report of the CSIS Commission on Cybersecurity for the 44th Presidency*, 3; U.S. Government Accountability Office, *Cybercrime: Public and Private Entities Face Challenges in Addressing Cyber Threats*, 33-34; Multi-State Information Sharing and Analysis Center, "About the MS-ISAC," http://www.msisac.org/about/ (accessed October 20, 2010).

163. Lynn, "Defending a New Domain," 97-109.

164. White House Office of the Press Secretary, "Remarks by the President on Securing our Nation's Cyber Infrastructure."

165. Pellerin, "Lynn: Cyberspace is the New Domain of Warfare."

166. Department of Homeland Security, *National Cyber Incident Response Plan-Interim Version* (Washington DC: Department of Homeland Security, September 2010), www.federalnewsradio.com/pdfs/NCIRP_Interim_Version_September_2010.pdf (accessed October 20, 2010).

167. Secretary of Homeland Security Janet Napolitano and Secretary of Defense Robert Gates, "Memorandum of Agreement Between The Department of Homeland Security and The Department of Defense Regarding Cybersecurity," September 27, 2010, http://www.dhs.gov/files/publications/gc_128 6986004190.shtm (accessed October 20, 2010).

168. Cheryl Pellerin, "DOD, DHS Join Forces to Promote Cybersecurity," American Forces Press Service, accessed on October 13, 2010, http://www.defense.gov/news/newsarticle. aspx?id=61264 (accessed October 20, 2010).

169. The Presidential Cybersecurity Coordinator is a Special Assistant to the President, serves primarily the President's representative to the interagency, and leads the interagency process for cyber security strategy and policy development. Like DHS, the Presidential Cybersecurity Coordinator has no. real authority to compel coordination, compliance, or action. See National Security Council, *Cybersecurity Progress after President Obama's Address*, July 14, 2010, http://www.whitehouse.gov/administration/eop/nsc/cybersecurity/progressreports/july2010 (accessed December 8, 2010); U.S. Government Accountability Office, *Cyberspace: United States Faces Challenges in Addressing Global Cybersecurity and Governance*, 7, 31, 33-34 & 41; Ellen Nakashima, "Obama to name Howard Schmidt as cybersecurity coordinator," *The Washington Post*, December 22, 2009, http://www.washingtonpost.com/wp-dyn/content/article/2009/12/21/AR2009122103055.html (accessed December 8, 2010).

170. Peter R. Orszag Director of the Office of Management and Budget and Howard A. Schmidt, Special Assistant to the President and Cybersecurity Coordinator, "Clarifying Cybersecurity Responsibilities and Activities of the Executive Office of the President and the Department of Homeland Security," Memorandum for the Heads of Executive Departments and Agencies," Washington, DC, July 6, 2010, http://www.whitehouse.gov/sites/default/files/omb/assets/memoranda_2010/m10-28.pdf (accessed December 8, 2010); Hollis, "USCYBERCOM: The Need for a Combatant Command versus a Subunified Command," 51-53.

171. Lynn, "Defending a New Domain," 97-109.

172. U.S. Government Accountability Office, *Cyberspace: United States Faces Challenges in Addressing Global Cybersecurity and Governance*, 33.

173. Russell Hsiao, "China's Cyber Command?"

174. Thomas Lum, *Internet Development and Information Control in the People's Republic of China* (Washington DC: U.S. Library of Congress, Congressional Research Service, February 10, 2006), 3; Clarke and Knake, *Cyber War: The Next Threat to National Security and What to Do About It*, 145-147; David Eimer, "How the Great Firewall of China keeps cyber dissidents in check," *The Independent*, November 16, 2005, http://www.independent.co.uk/news/world/asia/how-the-great-firewall-of-china-keeps-cyber-dissidents-in-check-515494.html (accessed December 8, 2010); Minxin Pei and Rebecca MacKinnon "Cyber-ocracy: How the Internet is Changing China," briefing presented at the Carnegie Endowment for International Peace, Washington DC, February 19, 2009, http://www.carnegieendowment.org/events/index.cfm?fa=eventDetail&id=1263 (accessed December 8, 2010); Art Jarmin, "Getting Around the Great Cyber Wall of China," *Internet Evolution*, March 10, 2009, http://www.internetevolution.com/author.asp?section_id=717&doc_id=173192 (accessed December 8, 2010).

175. Willy Lam, "Beijing beefs up cyber-warfare capacity," *The AsiaTimesOnline*, February 9, 2010, http://www.atimes.com/atimes/China/LB09Ad01.html (accessed November 25, 2010); Pei and MacKinnon "Cyber-ocracy: How the Internet is Changing China."

China's censorship of the anti-Mubarak demonstrations in Egypt is a recent example of PRC control of the internet. Early in the protests, China's web portals blocked keyword searches using the word "Egypt." When China's citizens attempted to use their version of Twitter, called Sina Weibo, to get news on Egypt, they received the message, "According to relevant laws, regulations and policies, the search results are not shown." Although the story was too big to expunge completely, the PRC directed national news media to run reports only from the state-run Xinhua News Agency. See Edward Wong and David Barboza, "Wary of Egypt Unrest, China Censors Web," *The New York Times*, January 31, 2011, http://www.nytimes.com/2011/02/01/world/asia/01beijing.html (accessed February 5, 2011); "Build a wall; China's reaction," *The Economist*, vol. 398, no. 8719, February 5, 2011, 34.

176. Lum, *Internet Development and Information Control in the People's Republic of China*, 4-7; Clarke and Knake, *Cyber War: The Next Threat to National Security and What to Do About It*, 145-147; Nina Hachigian, "China's cyber-strategy," *Foreign Affairs;* vol. 80, no. 2 (March/April 2001), 120-129, in ProQuest (accessed October 15, 2010).

177. Bill Gertz, "China blocks U.S. from cyber warfare," *The Washington Times*, May 12, 2009 http://www.washingtontimes.com/news/2009/may/12/china-bolsters-for-cyber-arms-race-with-us/print/ (accessed 20 October 2010).

178. From the Black Hat website: "The Black Hat Briefings are a series of highly technical information security conferences that bring together thought leaders from all facets of the infosec (*information security*) world – from the corporate and government sectors to academic and even underground researchers. The

environment is strictly vendor-neutral and focused on the sharing of practical insights and timely, actionable knowledge. Black Hat remains the best and biggest event of its kind, unique in its ability to define tomorrow's information security landscape. In addition to the large number of short, topical presentations in the Briefings, Black Hat also provides hands-on, high-intensity, multi-day Trainings. The Training sessions are provided by some of the most respected experts in the world and many also provide formal certifications to qualifying attendees. Arrangements can also be made to bring Black Hat's trainers to your location for private and customized training. Black Hat's decade of leadership attracts the most prestigious names from the full spectrum of security thinkers, and ensures that the conference stays on the leading edge of new security trends as they emerge. Our commitment to delegate feedback also helps keep our presentations aligned to the needs and desires of our delegates." See Black Hat, *About Black Hat Professional Security Events*, http://www.blackhat.com/html/about.html (accessed December 8, 2010).

179. Clarke and Knake, *Cyber War: The Next Threat to National Security and What to Do About It*, 130.

180. National Security Council, *The Comprehensive National Cybersecurity Initiative*.

181. Gates, *National Defense Strategy 2008*, 6-12.

182. Adams, "Virtual Defense," 98-112.

183. U.S. Government Accountability Office, *Cyberspace: United States Faces Challenges in Addressing Global Cybersecurity and Governance*, i-ii.

184. U.S. Government Accountability Office, *National Cybersecurity Strategy: Key Improvements Are Needed to Strengthen the Nation's Posture* (Washington DC: U.S. Government Accountability Office, March 10, 2009), 9.

185. About the Office of the Director of National Intelligence, http://www.dni.gov/who.htm (accessed December 8 2010).

186. National Security Council, *The Comprehensive National Cybersecurity Initiative*.

187. U.S. Government Accountability Office, *Cyberspace: United States Faces Challenges in Addressing Global Cybersecurity and Governance*, i-ii.

188. Lynn, "Defending a New Domain," 97-109.

189. National Security Council, *The Comprehensive National Cybersecurity Initiative*.

190. Ibid.

191. Gail H. Brooks, "Content Monitoring & Protection (CMP) as an OPSEC Compliance Tool," information paper prepared for Deputy Chief of Staff Army G-3/5/7 (DAMO-ODI), Fort Belvoir, Virginia, May 28, 2010.

192. Ben Bain, "DHS releases new details on Einstein 3 intrusion prevention pilot," *Federal Computer Week*, March 19, 2010, http://fcw.com/articles/2010/03/19/einstein-3-test-intrusion-prevention-system.aspx (accessed November 9, 2010);

Mary Ellen Callahan, *Privacy Impact Assessment for the Initiative Three Exercise* (Washington DC: Department of Homeland Security, March 18, 2010), 10-16, http://www.dhs.gov/xlibrary/assets/privacy/privacy_pia_nppd_initiative3 exercise.pdf (accessed October 20, 2010); Seamus K. Berry, "Legal Review for 1st IO Command Employment of Content Aware Critical Data Loss Prevention Appliances in support of Army OPSEC," memorandum for Deputy Chief of Staff Army G-3/5/7 (DAMO-ODI), August 23, 2010.

193. National Security Council, *The Comprehensive National Cybersecurity Initiative.*

194. "Websense, a provider of employee Internet management solutions, said that Internet misuse in the workplace costs American corporations more than $178 billion annually in lost productivity. This translates into a loss of more than $5,000 per employee, per year. Workplace Internet access continues to increase, resulting in more than 68 million U.S. employees accessing the web at work in 2005, according to the IDC Internet Commerce Market Model version 9.1. However, as web use becomes increasingly engaging and interactive, workers are spending more office time surfing the Internet for personal reasons. A recent America Online and Salary.com survey reported that 44.7% of the more than 10,000 American workers polled cited web surfing as their number one distraction at work. Furthermore, according to a recent Websense/Harris Interactive Web@Work survey, 50% of employees surveyed, who access the Internet at work, admit they do so for both work and personal reasons. Based upon this statistic, of the 68 million U.S. employees who access the Internet at work, approximately 34 million spend time surfing the web for personal usage at the office. This time spent 'cyberslacking', multiplied by the average U.S. salary, as reported by the US Bureau of Labor's National Compensation Survey, accounts for the multi-billion dollar crisis facing American businesses." See DQ Channels, *Internet misuse at workplace*, July 25, 2005 http://dqchannels.ciol. com/content/ reselleralert/105072503.asp (accessed December 8, 2010).

195. J. Nicholas Hoover, "Gen. Alexander Calls For 'Secure, Protected Zone' On Internet For Nation's Networks," *InformationWeek,* http://www.darkreading. com/security/government/show Article.jhtml?articleID=227500612 (accessed October 25, 2010).

196. Thom Shanker, "Cyberwar Chief Calls for Secure Computer Network," *The New York Times,* http://www.nytimes.com/2010/09/24/us/24cyber.html (accessed October 25, 2010).

197. S. Massoud Amin, "Securing the Electricity Grid," *The Bridge*, vol. 40, no. 1 (Spring 2010), 19-20; Peter D. Gasper, "Cyber Threat to Critical Infrastructure 2010-2015," 2-3.

198. John Markoff and David Barboza, "Academic Paper in China Sets Off Alarms in U.S.," *The New York Times*, March 20, 2010, http://www.nytimes. com/2010/03/21/world/asia/21grid.html (accessed November 25, 2010).

199. National Security Council, *The Comprehensive National Cybersecurity Initiative.*

200. Clarke and Knake, *Cyber War: The Next Threat to National Security and What to Do About It*, 140.

201. Ibid., 160-178.

202. National Security Council, *The Comprehensive National Cybersecurity Initiative*.

203. U.S. Government Accountability Office, *National Cybersecurity Strategy: Key Improvements Are Needed to Strengthen the Nation's Posture*, 9.

204. Department of Homeland Security, National Cybersecurity Awareness Month, http://www.dhs.gov/files/programs/gc_1158611596104.shtm (accessed December 10, 2010).

205. Inkster, "China in Cyberspace," 65; Clarke and Knake, *Cyber War: The Next Threat to National Security and What to Do About It*, 160-161.

206. National Security Council, *The Comprehensive National Cybersecurity Initiative*.

207. "Merkel's China Visit Marred by Hacking Allegations," *Spiegel Online International*; AFP, "China rejects US Web hijack allegations."

208. Shirley A. Kan, *U.S.-China Military Contacts: Issues for Congress* (Washington, DC: U.S. Library of Congress, Congressional Research Service, December 14, 2010), 3-4 & 18, http://opencrs.com/syndication/recent.xml (accessed on January 21, 2011).

209. Nye, *Cyber Power*, 16-17; Adams, "Virtual Defense," 98-112.

210. Thomas, *The Dragon's Quantum Leap: Transforming from a Mechanized to an Informatized Force*, 187; Shirley A. Kan, *U.S.-China Military Contacts :Issues for Congress*, 3-4, 18 & 34.

211. U.S. Congress, Senate, Senate Armed Services Committee, *Advance Questions for Lieutenant General Keith Alexander, USA, Nominee for Commander, United States Cyber Command*, 12; Secretary of State's International Security Advisory Board, *Report from the ISAB Task Force: China's Strategic Modernization*, 6-9.

Lieutenant General Keith Alexander, responding to questions from the Senate Armed Services Committee said, "The establishment of U.S. Cyber Command, in and of itself, does not change the lawful employment of military force for self-defense. In this case, if the 'attack' met the criteria approved by the President in our Standing Rules of Engagement, the military would exercise its obligation of self-defense. Operationally, it is difficult to develop an effective response when we do not know who is responsible for an 'attack'; however, the circumstances may be such that at least some level of mitigating action can be taken even when we are not certain who is responsible. Regardless whether we know who is responsible, international law requires that our use of force in self-defense be proportional and discriminate. Neither proportionality nor discrimination requires that we know who is responsible before we take defensive action."

212. Hathaway, *Cyberspace Policy Review: Assuring a Trusted and Resilient Information and Communications Infrastructure*; Hathaway, *National Strategy to Secure Cyberspace*.

213. U.S. Government Accountability Office, *Cyberspace: United States Faces Challenges in Addressing Global Cybersecurity and Governance*, 37-38.

214. Greg Masters, "Global cybercrime treaty rejected at U.N.," *SCMagazine*, April 23, 2010, http://www.scmagazineus.com/global-cybercrime-treaty-rejected-at-un/article/168630/ (accessed November 8, 2010); Mark Ballard, "UN rejects international cybercrime treaty *ComputerWeekly*," 20 April 2010, http://www.computerweekly.com/Articles/2010/04/20/ 240973/UN-rejects-international-cybercrime-treaty.htm (accessed November 8, 2010).

215. In addition to 47 members of the Council of Europe, ten other countries are signatory members of the *Convention*, including Argentina, Australia, Canada, Chile, Costa Rica, Dominican Republic, Japan, Mexico, Philippines, South Africa, and the United States. Council of Europe, *Convention on Cybercrime,* Chart of signatures and ratifications, status as of December 10, 2010, http://conventions.coe.int/Treaty/Commun/ChercheSig.asp?NT=185&CM =&DF= &CL=ENG (accessed December 10, 2010).

216. Brian Harley, "A Global Convention on Cybercrime?" *Columbia Science and Technology Law Review*, March 23, 2010, http://www.stlr.org/2010/03/a-global-convention-on-cybercrime/ (accessed November 8, 2010).

217. United Nations General Assembly Resolution 3314, *Definition of Aggression*, University of Minnesota – Human Rights Library, http://www1.umn.edu/humanrts/instree/GAres3314.html (accessed December 10, 2010).

218. The United Nations, *Charter of the United Nations*, Chapter VII: Action with Respect to Threats to the Peace, Breaches of the Peace, and Acts of Aggression, Article 41, http://www.un.org/en/documents/charter/chapter7.shtml (accessed December 10, 2010); Schaap, "The Development of Cyber Warfare Operations and Analysing Its Use Under International Law," 144.

219. U.S. Congress, Senate, Senate Armed Services Committee, *Advance Questions for Lieutenant General Keith Alexander, USA, Nominee for Commander, United States Cyber Command*, 12.

220. NATO is at least aware of the existing cyber threat, acknowledged in *NATO 2020: Assured Security; Dynamic Engagement,* a document which provides "analysis and recommendations of the group of experts on a New Strategic Concept" for the Alliance. Awareness does not necessarily translate into action, as the below list of six cyber related recommendations illustrates. See North Atlantic Treaty Organization, *NATO 2020: Assured Security; Dynamic Engagement,* May 17, 2010, 35, http://www.nato.int/strategic-concept/experts report.pdf (accessed January 14 2011).

"Cyber defence capabilities. The next significant attack on the Alliance may well come down a fibre optic cable. Already, cyber attacks against NATO systems

occur frequently, but most often below the threshold of political concern. However, the risk of a large-scale attack on NATO's command and control systems or energy grids could readily warrant consultations under Article 4 and could possibly lead to collective defence measures under Article 5. Effective cyber defence requires the means to prevent, detect, respond to, and recover from attacks. NATO has taken steps to develop these capabilities through creation of a Cyber Defence Management Authority, a Cooperative Cyber Defence Centre of Excellence, and a Computer Incident Response Capability. Nonetheless, there persist serious gaps in NATO's cyber defence capabilities. The Strategic Concept should place a high priority on addressing these vulnerabilities, which are both unacceptable and increasingly dangerous.

Recommendations:

1. NATO should recognize that cyber attacks are a growing threat to the security of the Alliance and its members. Accordingly:

- A major effort should be undertaken to increase the monitoring of NATO's critical network and to assess and furnish remedies to any vulnerabilities that are identified.

- The Centre of Excellence should do more, through training, to help members improve their cyber defence programmes.

- Allies should expand early warning capabilities in the form of a NATO-wide network of monitoring nodes and sensors.

- The Alliance should be prepared to send an expert team to any member experiencing or threatened by a major cyber attack.

- Over time, NATO should plan to mount a fully adequate array of cyber defence capabilities, including passive and active elements."

221. K. Alan Kronstadt, *India-U.S. Relations* (Washington DC: U.S. Library of Congress, Congressional Research Service, July 1, 2008), 18-19, 47. Also see updated version: K. Alan Kronstadt, *India-U.S. Relations* (Washington DC: U.S. Library of Congress, Congressional Research Service, January 30, 2009), 21-22 & 52.

222. U.S. Congress, Senate, Senate Armed Services Committee, *Advance Questions for Lieutenant General Keith Alexander, USA, Nominee for Commander, United States Cyber Command*, 32.

223. Inkster, "China in Cyberspace," 60.

224. Jake Tapper, et al., "No Mandarin Word for 'Town Hall': Obama Introduces China to US Political Tradition," *ABC News*, November 16, 2009, http://abcnews.go.com/Politics/president-obama-holds-town-hall-china-human-rights/story?id=9091246 (accessed October 25, 2010).

225. Secretary of State's International Security Advisory Board, *Report from the ISAB Task Force: China's Strategic Modernization*, 1.

226. Mulvenon, "PLA Computer Network Operations: Scenarios, Doctrine, Organizations, and Capability," 260-271; Mulvenon, "The PLA and Information Warfare," 180-85; Jan van Tol, et al., *Air Sea Battle: A Point-of-Departure Operational Concept* (Washington DC: Center for Strategic and Budgetary Assessments, 2010), ix-xii, 18-22.

227. Nye, *Cyber Power*, 10-11; Mark Clayton, "Stuxnet 'virus' could be altered to attack US facilities, report warns," *The Christian Science Monitor*, December 15, 2010, http://www. csmonitor.com/USA/2010/1215/Stuxnet-virus-could-be-altered-to-attack-US-facilities-report-warns (accessed December 19, 2010).

228. Audrey Plonk and Anne Carblanc, *Malicious Software (Malware): A Security Threat to the Internet Economy* (Paris, France: Organization for Economic Co-operation and Development, March 6, 2008), 10-32, http://www.oecd.org/dataoecd/53/34/40724457.pdf (accessed November 28, 2010).